Barry Hannah

Twayne's United States Authors Series

Frank Day, Editor

Clemson University

TUSAS 593

Barry Hannah

Mark J. Charney

Clemson University

Twayne Publishers • New York
Maxwell Macmillan Canada • Toronto
Maxwell Macillan International • New York Oxford Singapore Sydney

For my wife, Sappho and my best friend, Jim

Barry Hannah
Mark J. Charney

Twayne Publishers
Macmillan Publishing Company
866 Third Avenue
New York, New York 10022

Maxwell Macmillan Canada, Inc.
1200 Eglinton Avenue East
Suite 200
Don Mills, Ontario M3C 3N1

Macmillan Publishing Company is part of the Maxwell Communications
Group of Companies.

10 9 8 7 6 5 4 3 2 1

The paper used in this publication meets the minimum requirements
of American National Standard for Information Sciences—Permanence
of Paper for Printed Library Materials, ANSI Z39.48-1984. ∞™

Printed and bound in the United States of America.

Library of Congress Cataloging-in-Publication Data

Charney, Mark J.
    Barry Hannah / Mark J. Charney.
        p.   cm. — (Twayne's United States authors series ; TUSAS 593)
    Includes bibliographical references and index.
    ISBN 0-8057-7633-8
    1. Hannah, Barry—Criticism and interpretation. I. Title.
II. Series.
PS3558.A476Z6   1991
811'.54—dc20
                                            91-31018
                                              CIP

Contents

Preface

This is the first full-length critical study of the work of Barry Hannah, one of the South's most refreshing and original writers. Winner of the Bellaman Foundation Award in Fiction, the Arnold Gingrich Short Fiction Award, and the William Faulkner Prize for Creative Writing, Hannah is the author of six novels and two collections of stories. The honesty of his vision and variety of his narrative voices have been compared to the best of the Southern canon, including Mark Twain, William Faulkner, Eudora Welty, and Flannery O'Connor.

My study of Barry Hannah examines his progression as a fiction writer and describes his experiments with language, voice, and form. I correlate Hannah's literary themes and techniques with the influences shaping his life. In each chapter I summarize the primary criticism of two novels or one collection of short stories, pointing to thematic and structural innovations. I also relate the many "voices" Hannah assumes to biographical information that has influenced his choice of characters and actions.

I have organized the book chronologically to illustrate Hannah's growing preoccupation with unconventional narrative form and to delineate the thematic shift from violence and isolation to peaceful alternatives and community acceptance. Chapter 1 discusses Hannah's use of multiperspectivism in his first two novels, *Geronimo Rex* and *Nightwatchmen,* and demonstrates the tension that Hannah creates between autobiography and fiction, between honesty and falsehood, which drives his fiction and unifies his work.

In chapter 2 I examine several of the stories from *Airships* to illustrate the variety of narrative voices and the similarities of the crises that render the narrators unable to act. I also define characteristics of these 20 stories to show that *Airships* reflects a unified vision of the South and a microcosm for human existence.

Chapter 3 introduces the themes of randomness and disjunctiveness in Hannah's fiction, illustrated by his experiments with fragmentary experience in *Ray* and *The Tennis Handsome.* I suggest that this new narrative formlessness increases the theme of violence that runs through the early works by making the characters' excessive, bizarre actions appear casual and unexpected.

In chapter 4 I discuss the seven stories of *Captain Maximus* as they represent Hannah's characters' need for peaceful alternatives to replace the violence of the past and present. I also illustrate Hannah's technique of paralleling cinematic montage in the experimental story "Power and Light" (a treatment for film).

In the final chapter I explore Hannah's use of first-person narration and oral tradition in *Hey Jack!* and *Boomerang* to unite vignettes uninhibited by conventional spatial and temporal narrative restrictions. Although the two novels are very different, both juxtapose seemingly unrelated tales to describe a town's heritage and to uncover the need for strong communal ties.

Charles Israel, in the *Dictionary of Literary Biography,* compares Hannah to William Faulkner: "Like his Mississippi brother in letters, Hannah uses the South as microcosm. In his fiction, the South, its people, its traditions, its social ills, and its violence, all become emblems of the human condition" (131). Hannah may write primarily about his experiences in the South, but his experiments with prose and the variety of his voices are not restricted to region. His works explore the human psyche not only to determine why people are drawn to violent alternatives, but, more importantly, to illustrate that the need for communal acceptance ultimately overcomes the immediate gratification of violent impulses. It is my hope that this book will serve as an introduction to the works of a writer who promises to remain one of the South's freshest, most iconoclastic voices.

Acknowledgments

I would like to thank G. W. Koon, who encouraged me to accept this project and offered me support during its completion. I also appreciate the advice offered by readers Frank Day, Liz Fowler, and Barbara Sutton and the help Betsy Dendy provided in compiling the index. Thanks also go to the English Department at Clemson University and the Department of Liberal Arts for encouraging faculty members to pursue their individual research interests and to Judy Payne, Pearl Parker, and Kim Hunter for their kindness, efficiency, and support over the last few years.

Chronology

1942   Barry Hannah born 23 April in Clinton, Mississippi, son of William and Elizabeth (King) Hannah.

1960   Enters Mississippi College in Clinton.

1964   Graduates with B.A. from Mississippi College; enters M.A. program in English at the University of Arkansas.

1966   Graduates with M.A. from the University of Arkansas.

1967   Graduates with M.F.A. from the Creative Writing Program at the University of Arkansas; begins teaching literature and creative writing at Clemson University in South Carolina (through 1973).

1970   Receives Bellaman Foundation Award in Fiction.

1971   Receives Bread Loaf Fellowship for Writing.

1972   *Geronimo Rex*. Awarded William Faulkner Prize for Writing. Nominated for National Book Award.

1973   *Nightwatchmen*.

1974   Writer-in-residence at Middlebury College, Vermont (until 1975).

1975   Begins teaching literature and fiction writing at the University of Alabama (until 1980).

1978   *Airships*. Awarded Arnold Gingrich Short Fiction Award.

1979   Award for literature from the American Institute of Arts and Letters.

1980   Moves to Hollywood to write film scripts for director Robert Altman; *Ray*.

1981   Writer-in-residence at the University of Iowa, Iowa City.

1982   Writer-in-residence at the University of Mississippi in Oxford.

1983   Writer-in-residence at the University of Montana-Missoula, then back to the University of Mississippi; *The Tennis Handsome*.

1985   *Captain Maximus*.

1987   *Hey Jack!*

1989   *Boomerang*.

Chapter One

The Autobiographical and the Violent: *Geronimo Rex* and *Nightwatchmen*

In an interview with R. Vanarsdall for the *Southern Review,* Hannah cited his innovative and controversial use of autobiography as a primary factor distinguishing his work from that of other Southern writers: "They remain obsessed by autobiography, but I use it as a mode to get to the real stuff which is almost always lying."[1] Although often compared to William Faulkner and Eudora Welty on the basis on his Southern heritage, Hannah admires those writers who reinvent autobiographical information in creative fictional form: "The people I like are looser and fuller like [Henry] Miller and [Thomas] Wolfe" (Vanarsdall, 339). In his first two novels, *Geronimo Rex* (1970) and *Nightwatchmen* (1973), Hannah uses autobiographical incident as a catalyst to encourage an imaginative response rather than as a means to convey or relive personal history. Believing that good writing stems naturally from experience, he uses elements of his own life during and after the writing of one novel directly to inspire the focus of his next: "The main part of my stories always comes out of life. I'm terribly affected by something, obsessed with it, or find it a situation I can't forget, and then the rest is imagination. But the emotional part is always something I've been through."[2] From his experience, Hannah draws the emotional honesty that drives his characters to act; from his imagination, he discovers the most appropriate framework to express the motivation and inspiration for these actions.

Born in Clinton, Mississippi, on 23 April 1942, son of insurance agent William Hannah and his wife Elizabeth King Hannah, Barry grew up in Mississippi, Alabama, and Louisiana. Not until he entered the master of arts program in English at the University of Arkansas in 1964 (after earning his B. A. at Mississippi College) did Hannah seriously consider writing as a career. After completing the M.A., Hannah pursued a master of fine arts degree in creative writing at Arkansas, inspired by three professors at the university: Bill Harrison, Ben Kimpel, and Jim Whitehead. Harrison introduced Hannah to his first agent; Kimpel introduced him to European literature; and Whitehead, the poet from Mississippi, taught Hannah that a love of poetry and fiction does not lessen one's masculinity. "In the South there's always a touch of the sissy about the arts," Hannah admitted in 1984. "Jim was an ex-football player. I was impressed that this brawny man gave a damn about his sonnets, and I got very serious" (Gretland, 232).

After graduating from the University of Arkansas with both M. A. and M. F. A. degrees in 1966, Hannah began teaching literature and creative writing at Clemson University in South Carolina. In 1968 his short story "The Crowd Punk-Season Drew" was published in the first issue of *Intro* (1968), an annual journal featuring fiction from the nation's writing programs. Hannah would use "The Crowd Punk-Season Drew" as the inspiration for his first novel, *Geronimo Rex*.

Geronimo Rex: The Violent Implications of Lying

In a study of *Geronimo Rex* David Madden writes of the similarities between author and protagonist: "So even though Barry, like Harry, plays the trumpet and went to school in Mississippi and Arkansas, the novel, which begins in 1950 when author and character were eight years old, is not slavishly autobiographical."[3] Hannah places *Geronimo Rex* (1970) within the tradition of such writers as Faulkner, Welty, O'Connor, and Wolfe by emphasizing the influence of the South upon a series of grotesque, eccentric, and violent characters. He also attempts to record the struggle of the individual to assert his independence in a community that fosters violence by resisting any change that breaks from tradition and the past. But the originality of his vision lies in his reinterpretation of autobiography to suit his own paradoxical purposes: Hannah begins with the truth, as he judges it from personal experience, to uncover the violent implications of lying.

A bildungsroman, similar in structure to such novels as *The Catcher in the Rye, Geronimo Rex* traces its protagonist, Harriman Monroe, from age 8 in Dream of Pines, Louisiana, to age 23 when he is newly married and enrolled in the graduate English program at the University of Arkansas. Hannah divides the novel into three sections: the first follows Harry through his senior year in high school, the second explores Harry's adventures at the fictional Hedermansever College in Mississippi, and the third spans the period from his senior year at college to the beginning of his graduate program at Arkansas.

In his review of *Geronimo Rex* in the *New Yorker,* John Updike likens the novel and its discontented protagonist to an older tradition, "the whining adolescent novel of the fifties":[4] "The youth of the fifties were not, as is sometimes implied, complacent; their contempt for the institutions around them was paralyzingly thorough. Salinger's Holden Caulfield, Keith Waterhouse's Billy Liar saw right through everything, and were too savvy to believe things could ever be otherwise" (Updike, 123). Like Holden and Billy, Harry searches actively and angrily to find a sense of belonging and a reason to exist, but unlike such novels of the fifties, *Geronimo Rex* is almost picaresque in its episodic organization and surreal in its exploitation of violence.

Geronimo Rex met with almost unanimous critical praise. Jim Harrison in the *New York Times Book Review* wrote that Hannah's first novel was "a stunning piece of entertainment, almost a totally successful book,"[5] and David Madden believes that the book "remains [13 years after his initial reading and review] the best first novel I have reviewed" (Madden, 309). The novel won Hannah the Bellaman Foundation and the William Faulkner awards for fiction. It was also nominated for the National Book Award.

David Madden attributes much of the success of *Geronimo Rex* to the mature first-person style Hannah adopts in the extensive revision of "The Crowd Punk-Season Drew": "The early sophomoric cuteness of 'The Crowd Punk-Season Drew' has been transmuted into a mature wittiness. Hannah made an intelligent decision when he shifted from the third to the first person, in which his inventive style works much more brilliantly. And he was wise to drop his hero's conscious image of himself as a cowardly punk" (Madden, 309). Hannah's decision to adopt a first-person narrator in *Geronimo Rex* lends the novel an intimacy not present in the short story upon which it was based. With the exception of a few short stories and a screenplay, Hannah continued to write most of his early fiction using the first-person narrative convention. As he explained to Jan Gretland in an interview for *Contemporary Authors,* "I can occasionally write short stories where I venture into the third person. But for long-distance writing, I count on basic honesty and a hot moment. I don't seem to go for very long with a character who's completely out of myself. I can't sustain it" (Gretland, 234). First-person narration, according to Hannah, is his only method of obtaining a "base of emotion" from which he creates satire, humor, and irony.

But although Hannah relies on a traditional narrator to describe his adventures, the structure he chooses purposely lacks the conventional, chronological continuity of most bildungsroman novels. Hannah achieves continuity, for example, not by leading the reader logically or smoothly from one event to another, but by introducing an array of minor characters who serve as foils to define Harry at various stages of his emotional and intellectual growth. Although many of the characters reappear throughout the book, Hannah describes most in terms of specific and discrete episodes. Rather than illustrate his progress toward maturity through a succession of didactic "lessons," Hannah indicates changes in Harry's perspective by describing achronologically his shifting behavior during each segment and his unpredictable reactions to other characters in the novel.

The primary foil in book 1, for example, is Harley Butte, the Sousa-loving, mulatto bandsman who works at Harry's father's mattress factory in Dream of Pines, where he even hears music in the making of bedsprings: "The Mulatto really had nothing against making mattress frames. . . . Harley liked to hear the music of hammers and springs, and he liked to see the mattresses take shape through the glass where the women were working with sewing machines alongside his area."[6] In book 1 Harry's reaction to Butte progresses from jealous amusement to respect and admiration. As Butte continues to reappear throughout the novel, Harry's respect for him becomes violent and defensive; it is almost as if Harry must defend Butte against the prejudice of others to exercise him from his (Harry's) own.

Violence eventually become Harry's preferred method of challenging anyone whom he believes wrongs Butte. In " 'Fight Fight! Nigger and a White!' " (chapter 7 of book 2), for example, Harry receives an invitation to see Butte's Beta Camina High School (Colored) Marching and Concert Band perform on Capitol Street in Jackson, Mississippi. He decides to bring a pistol to the parade after reading an incendiary letter in the Jackson newspaper written by his nemesis Peter Lepoyster. "Whitfield Peter," so-called after his sojourn in Whitfield Asylum, castigates the voodoo sewage, cooties, lice, and "fleamales" supposedly resulting from the "Afracoon" band's appearance in Mississippi. When Peter reaches for a handkerchief during the Beta Camina Band concert at the parade, Harry wants to assume that Peter plans to assassinate Butte: "I knew he was going for a gun; it did not occur to me that he could be reaching for anything but a gun, my forehead was hot with knowing this. . . . I already had mine out and was already to the middle of the street since I knew I could hit nothing from the distance I was from the sidewalk" (*Rex*, 190). When the opportunity for violence fails to materialize, Harry is actually disappointed. At this point in his life, Harry romantically sees himself as a twentieth-century warrior, ready to defend Butte's honor even if the musician would prefer *not* to be defended. Butte himself carries little significance in the scene as a character or even as a plot device; his two other reappearances in the novel signal and encourage the violence within Harry stemming from his own inability to eliminate totally the in-bred Southern prejudice within himself.

Other characters in *Geronimo Rex* illustrate Hannah's method of defining Harry. In college, Robert (Bobby) Dove Fleece, Harry's college roommate and a self-proclaimed genius, and Peter Lepoyster become the central foils for illustrating aspects of Harry's progression toward manhood. An initial meeting with Fleece prompts Harry to call him a "flit" and halfheartedly consider physical abuse: "I really didn't want to crush the boy. Right now I could see my fist go into his head as into a cantaloupe, and there was no victory in it" (*Rex*, 141). In spite of his effeminacy and genteel background, Fleece ultimately becomes Harry's friend, accomplice, and even romantic mentor. Fleece's baroque prose and persuasive rhetoric influence Harry to perceive the music and eloquence of the written and spoken word. Although it is Fleece's initial prodding that convinces Harry to attend medical school, his love of language and romantic vision of the world ironically influence Harry to pursue a career in liberal arts.

Harry, in turn, serves as a mentor for Fleece as well; he teaches Fleece the benefits of violence, especially in sexual relationships. Imitating Harry's behavior, Fleece shoots one of his roommates, Silas, when Silas begins dating Fleece's girl, Bet. As the two become better friends, Fleece becomes more like Harry: his relationships with women grow increasingly unbalanced and he is attracted to violence.

Unlike Harley Butte, however, Fleece also serves as a strong plot device. He introduces Harry to "Whitfield" Peter Lepoyster, for whom Harry conceives such a hatred that he is driven to his most obsessive, violent, and romantic behavior. On a high school trip to Madison County, Fleece locates and steals pornographic letters that Peter had written to his wife Catherine before her untimely death during their honeymoon. The letters reveal Peter's impassioned and compulsive love for Catherine and his hatred for anyone who is not white, Christian, and southern: "They [the Jews] will raise up the nigger and teach him power and pride of position, and somehow too they will have to deal with that barbarous voodoo 'christianity,' and they will fail. . . . I am pointed to action: TO TREAT EVERY NIGGER AS IF HE WERE A JEW AND EVERY JEW AS IF HE WERE A NIGGER" (*Rex*, 152). Although Harry externally detests Peter's narrow-minded distrust of all that is unfamiliar, he envies in Peter his compulsive and all-consuming love for his wife and his niece. Hannah uses the episodes with Peter to illustrate Harry's inability to dedicate himself to any one goal or relationship. Harry, much like Hannah himself, wavers in his career ambitions, from medical to pharmaceutical to musical to academic vocations, as often as he shifts from one woman to the next. He does not understand what drives the single-minded Peter to act; so, ironically, he reacts to Peter much like Peter would like to react to blacks and Jews: with violence.

Although David Madden believes that "Peter is Hannah's most magnificent creation, more a product of his imagination, one hopes, than any of his other characters" (Madden, 313), Hannah based the character on familiar Mississippi types he had encountered in his youth. In his interview with Jan Gretland, he stated that "anybody in Mississippi who's my age or older will tell you that such a character is hardly an invention. I grew up reading letters in the paper down in Jackson that weren't too far off from the letters I wrote for *Geronimo Rex*" (Gretland, 233). And to R. Vanarsdall Hannah admitted that Peter's letters "came from some real letters that we discovered around an old house in Rodney, Mississippi, apparently from an inmate at Whitfield to his love" (Vanarsdall, 319). Although he did not have the letters in front of him while he wrote, he remembered their "European, baroque, and pornographic" content and style when he composed Peter's correspondence.

But Harry's fear of Peter and his hatred for the prejudice exhibited in his letters do not prevent him from subconsciously admiring Peter as a romantic Southern icon. Peter influences Harry as much as Fleece does, especially in relation to women. Before he meets Fleece and Peter, Harry reacts to women on a desperate sexual and emotional level. His first high school dreamgirl, Ann Mick, for example, illustrates Harry's youth and sexual inexperience. A girl with a shady reputation (she is rumored to have given birth to a basketball player's child), Ann represents Harry's infatuation with the idea of being in love. Maintaining a dream relationship with her is ultimately more important and desirable than establishing a realistic relationship: "I tried hard to dream about her again and get her to give me some message in the dream, but I couldn't. The memory of her in the dream was waning, and I got in a desperate funk" (*Rex*, 52). Not until he realizes that his own father holds a similar infatuation for Ann does he abandon dreams of transforming the girl's life through the power of love and money. And, of course, after the infatuation dies, Harry thinks primarily of her violent and fiery demise: "and Ann tangled up with her current lover in the back seat of a car parked in her front yard, Ann on fire like a building, with her ribs broiling in my X-ray view, and the guy she was with screeching as his crotch turned to embers and flames took his head" (*Rex*, 71).

Harry's relationships with women before he attends college build his ego and further his limited sexual experience. While attending a summer music institute in New York, he has an affair with Sylvia Wyche, a "technical virgin" from North Carolina who seduces Harry, but wants to protect her hymen for her fiancé, Charles. In Dream of Pines, he takes Tonnie Ray Reese to the prom, where she vomits on him during his attempt at seduction. A senior who imagines that Harry holds the secret to maintaining her popularity and sense of importance even after graduation, Tonnie Ray never holds real interest for Harry. He dates her primarily to improve his high school reputation and to alleviate rumors of his homosexuality. Meanwhile, he longs for Lala Sink, daughter of Dream of Pines's wealthiest family. In college, he has a brief affair with Bonnie, a girl from Holly Springs with polio in one leg, "a regular witch at murdering love" who seduces an array of men involved in serious relationships (*Rex,* 132).

But after reading Peter's pornographic letter to his wife and seeing the man's obsessive, almost incestuous love for his white-trash niece renamed Catherine (after Peter's deceased wife), Harry modifies his view of relationships, and, in turn, his idea of love. Although he still falls occasionally into liaisons purely for selfish and sexual gratification, such as the one-night stand with Patsy, the flute player in the Jackson symphony who is attracted to the ugliness of the male torso, he begins to ask out Peter's niece Catherine to fulfill his newly formed image of romantic commitment. For two years he pursues Catherine, attracted more by her lovely appearance and her enigmatic association with her deceased aunt than to her inferior mind and lack of grammatical ability, without once attempting to further their relationship physically: "It caused me no special anguish to resist. I heard Peter's voice in my mind while I was with her, but that isn't why I was so chaste" (*Rex,* 273). Ultimately, Harry realizes that he easily maintains a chaste relationship with Catherine because his love for her is inspired more by imitation of Peter's depth of feeling and Fleece's romantic ideal of love than his own. The romance, therefore, is inevitably a false one: "she was just a roach, after all. I knew the breed better than any. . . . My dozen nights with her never approached romance, never approached *anything.* It would've been the same if I'd picked her up on the street. I had never met a roach that I couldn't get a good bit of my marvelous self across to" (*Rex,* 273). Ironically, it is during his final afternoon with Catherine that he experiences a "butterfly of sentiment," an affection for her naive vulnerability that he cannot shake. But true to Harry's nature, since he does not understand this strange interlude or his feelings for Catherine, he strives to forget his affection before he is defeated by it: "I was absorbed for days in trying to forget the afternoon. . . . I knew if I thought of it too much more, it would fall around my neck like a noose and hang me" (*Rex,* 308). Harry longs to share the depth of Peter's and Fleece's emotional commitment, but he continues to run from feelings not easily accessible within his patterns of behavior.

Fleece and Peter also help to inspire in Harry a romanticized view of violence. Harry has always been attracted to violence, but with Fleece and Peter he begins to justify it as a means to achieve morality. His friendship with Fleece and his rivalry with Peter encourage Harry to idealize his own quest for love and righteousness. The associations he affects between himself and the Indian Geronimo (who gives the novel its title) illustrate this shift in Harry's view of violence. At Hedermansever's library, he discovers the exploits of Geronimo and begins to parallel the personality of the Indian with what he views as his own true nature: "What I especially liked about Geronimo then was that he had cheated, lied, stolen, mutinied, usurped, killed, burned, raped, pillaged, razed, trapped, ripped, mashed, bowshot, stomped, herded, exploded, cut, stoned, revenged, prevenged, avenged, and was his own man" (*Rex,* 231). David Madden explains this identification with Geronimo and this love of violence as a stage of adolescence: "All of these means and expressions of power—the ready pistol, the intimidating costume, the dirty fighting, the identification with Geronimo, the trumpet blasting—are adolescent techniques for mental survival" (Madden, 311). Donald R. Noble, in " 'Tragic and Meaningful to an Insane Degree': Barry Hannah," believes that this need for violence reflects an insecurity and paranoia about the world outside of the self: "Gratuitous or not, Hannah's characters feel the need to go armed in a world that they understandably perceive as extremely dangerous, although one might argue that it is in fact people like Hannah's characters that make this world such a dangerous place."[7]

Hannah defends his use of violence in novels such as *Geronimo Rex* by pointing out that it causes people to act more honestly: "I find people more animated when they have a gun to their heads. And I like people in situations of stress, because they tend to be frank and cheat less. . . . I'm not violent myself. And it is not that I have discovered effecting a revenge in my fiction that I can't get in the real world. I just frankly enjoy violence. I find it cathartic. . . . Denying violence altogether is a mistake" (Gretland, 234). Harry believes that because the world is already a dangerous place, characters must act offensively to ward off immediate and potential evil; therefore, he carries a gun, assuming that violence is inevitable, and waits for the anger in others to surface. Geronimo serves as Harry's symbol of the violence that is not only realistic, but also necessary for survival.

Geronimo appears to Harry's imagination as a genie, giving advice about dress, carriage, and behavior, and Harry begins to justify his own violent nature by comparing his exploits and fantasies to those of the Indian. Geronimo eventually even becomes the voice of Harry's moral conscience, distinguishing the necessary from the unnecessary, the significant from the petty. Ashamed by the manner in which he ends his relationship with Catherine, for example, Harry hears the betrayed voice of Geronimo threatening to leave him because of the pettiness of his behavior; ultimately, the threat of Geronimo's desertion encourages him to see Catherine again and to treat her more honorably.

Geronimo is a suitable choice of symbol for Harry because the immature Mississippian sees himself as a noble savage pursuing an often indefinable quest. Harry admires the idea of Geronimo's reputed six wives, his battles with the Mexicans who murdered his first wife and three children, his legendary rides across the Rio Grande and Arizona border, even "that the name Geronimo translated as 'one who belches' or 'one who yawns' or both at the same time" (*Rex,* 231). He admits to himself, "I would like to go into that line of work. I would like to leave behind me a gnashing horde of bastards" (*Rex,* 232). But the figure of Geronimo also illustrates the inequities in Harry's comparison between himself and the Indian. A Southerner who finds his traditions threatened, Harry may see himself as the wronged and noble survivor of a similarily ill-treated people, but because his real-life actions do not preserve this broken tradition, readers judge him much less sympathetically.

Robert W. Hill describes Harriman Monroe as a character who "draws our sympathy and distaste—we don't just feel that he is fatally caught in a loser's body; he seems especially to deserve it, if only for his postured eccentricity."[8] David Madden is harsher in his assessment of Harry. He calls the youth a "repulsively fascinating character" and finds especially distasteful Harry's unsuccessful pretense of nonconformity: "There is nothing drabber than the sight of a fundamental conformist indulging in feeble, often sneaky, acts that he celebrates as acts of rebellion or free-spiritedness" (Madden, 310). Although Madden writes that the author's own opinion of Harry is unclear, he believes audiences root for Harry because Hannah's appealing narrative voice makes readers unwilling accomplices (Madden, 311). Harry's actions certainly tend to alienate readers who expect a conventional, sympathetic protagonist with whom they can identify. In one of the first images of second grader Harriman Monroe, Hannah graphically describes the gratuitous murder of a neighbor's peacock: "The old boy was roosting about four feet off the ground this time and jumped on me at head level, making a loud racket in the cane as he launched himself. This terrified me, but I stood still and swung on the peacock with both arms. I caught him in the head and his beak swerved like plastic. He dropped on the bricks like a club, his fantail all folded in. I toed him. He was dead, with an eye wiped away" (*Rex*, 19). Throughout the novel, Hannah makes it clear that the slaughtered peacock (featured on the cover of paperback editions of *Geronimo Rex*) is a more appropriate symbol for Harry than the Indian he adapts as his cohort and mentor. In fact, recurrent, vividly described scenes of violence, inspired if not enacted by Harry, consistently remind readers of the true nature of the protagonist.

For example, he throws illegal and dangerous M-80 Salute Firecrackers (compared to small sticks of dynamite) at Harley Butte in a black bar to complete his self-proclaimed mission of "indefinite evil," and he fantasizes about lodging "one up the skirt of the school librarian and watch[ing] her rave off in pain and smoke" (*Rex*, 35). He hits a 12- or 13-year-old Lloyd Reese in the mouth to force the boy to give him trumpet lessons: "I hit him a couple of times and sure enough, he got quiet. . . . His tiny pointed knee-caps showed under his pants; his uniform was covered with wet grass crud" (*Rex*, 66). He shoots at small birds—"robins, sparrows, thrushes"—and threatens Peter and his niece Catherine by shooting aimlessly at their home, indirectly causing the fiery destruction of Peter's Pontiac (*Rex*, 169). He even encourages Fleece to shoot Peter in the kneecaps and is partially re-sponsible for influencing Silas, a fellow border, to hit Catherine in the face with a half-eaten apple.

Harry's consistent acts of violence ultimately drive the crazed Peter to wound Fleece and kill Mother Rooney, the boy's landlady, in an effort to avenge what is left of his home and honor. Inspired by the resurrected ghost of Geronimo, Harry attempts to kill the broken and unhappy Peter in the last chapter of the novel, but is successful only at sending him back to Whitfield Asylum, maimed and mute for the rest of his life: "He staggered away, examining me. His face was a horror: a mask of bruises all yellow and purple like hematomas. His eyesockets seemed to have been mauled and crushed. His lips were folded in-ward. He had lost his false teeth. He began that curious squeaky voice, the voice of a cartoon rodent" (*Rex*, 378). Hannah describes Harry throughout *Geronimo Rex* as a casual and thought-less harbinger of violence. Unlike his hero Geronimo, Harry attacks only those less strong and well-armed than himself. He foolishly proclaims that he fights fair and honorably, but because he packs a pistol and is almost al-ways on the offensive, the nobility of his violent quests and cruel outbursts is questionable.

What redeems Harry and illustrates at least a potential for sensitivity and thoughtfulness is his affection for his father, his sense of self-absurdity, and his depth of thought. He constantly compares his father, Ode Elann Monroe, to Humphrey Bogart and Jack Paar, and he labels him a "puller of the trigger when the chips were down" (*Rex,* 27). Genuinely bewildered when an off-color joke he hears at Hedermansever College alienates him from his dad, Harry regretfully admits, "Since then, very little has passed between us except money" (*Rex,* 171). He often worries about his father's opinion of him, and, although they disagree, Harry takes his father's advice seriously.

Harry finds humor not only in others' eccentricities, but especially in his own, from the ugliness of his torso to the reputation he earns of being a "desperate queer" in high school (*Rex,* 68). He even laughs when Tonnie Ray vomits on him during an aborted sexual attempt; while wearing her glasses he observes, "It was unbearable that I had Tonnie Ray's muck on me. But it was so beautiful not to be seeing Tonnie Ray clearly. And the world of these thick glasses was rather delightful" (*Rex,* 107). Ironically, Harry applies the same casual attitude toward violence to moments of self-recognition. After completely thrashing a high school student who calls him names, Harry confesses, "My fists hung down throbbing and there were tears in my eyes. I don't think I was meant to be a fighter" (*Rex,* 73). In spite of his often tough, insensitive, and bigoted position toward women, blacks, and southerners, he illustrates moments of true and moving sensitivity that draw the reader to him. Visiting the cemetery at Vicksburg full of Civil War casualties with Fleece, for example, Harry is overwhelmed by the memories and the range of emotions he encounters: "Jesus mercy, I was sad. We went and saw the last sight, a football-field-sized green full of white gravel blocks no more than six inches apart. . . . By then I was drooling blue. . . . The strange *silence,* then, is what got me—as if you walked in a dream of refracted defeat. The horror was, I could think of nothing to say" (*Rex,* 218). Hannah counters the reader's distaste for Harry's love of violence by heightening elements of the novel that describe the depth of his soul and the complexity of his insight; many incidents in the novel illustrate that Harry cares for more than just himself.

Most indicative of this depth and ability to transcend concern with the self is the music that begins and ends the novel. Although he immaturely celebrates the beauty and benefit of violence, through music Harry exhibits a love for art and an understanding of the soul. The novel begins with the eight-year-old Harry admiring the perfection of the Dream of Pines's "spade" band, in which Harley Butte plays the French horn. The music taps an enigmatic chord in the young southerner, one that he ironically associates with what he knows best—violence: "The way it was affecting me, I guess I was already a musician at the time and didn't know it. This band was the best music I'd ever heard, bar none. They made you want to pick up a rifle and just get killed somewhere. What drums, and what a wide brassy volume; and the woodwinds were playing tempestuously shrill. The trombones and tubas went deeper than what my heart had room for" (*Rex,* 14). This emotional and spiritual reaction to music influences Harry to learn the trumpet and to strive for the perfection of the Dream of Pines High School Band. But although Harry excels at the trumpet, because he is unable to capture either the beauty or the magic of Butte's band, he denies himself the pleasure of the instrument. In college, for example, Harry successfully forms a band that eventually becomes good enough to open for the popular Mean Men from Memphis. Although his band is well received by the audience, Harry imagines himself in front of Harley Butte's faultless Beta Camina Band playing perfect Sousa music: "I did not want to get sappy about this, did not want to *think,* aw God, but I felt shoddy, unrehearsed. . . . I knew I had been at the peak of what I wanted, I might still be on the peak, but I couldn't, *couldn't*" (*Rex,* 227). Harry realizes during this musical stint that his best actual music performance will never equal the spiritual one inspired by Butte, so he abandons the profession he admires most.

Geronimo Rex ends with Harry inexplicably married to 17-year-old Prissy Lombarde from Pascagoula, Mississippi, and enrolled in the graduate program in English at the University of Arkansas. But it is once again music, not marriage or career, that inspires within Harry the desire to reach, understand, and achieve perfection. In the last scene of the novel Harry takes Dr. Lariat, the professor who witnesses the shooting of Peter Lepoyster, to hear Harley Butte's Beta Camina Marching Band. Like Harry, Lariat is overwhelmed by the band's sound and appearance: "Would you listen to that. . . . They are superb. That is the best" (*Rex,* 318). Instead of playing the traditional Sousa marches, however, the band is playing Butte's own music: driven by the perfection he recognizes in Sousa, Harley is finally able to compose music.

This act of creation inspires Lariat in the last speech of the novel to tell Harry, "That *was* it. Good, good heavens. We're in the wrong field. Music!" (*Rex,* 381). Harry realizes at the end of *Geronimo Rex* that it is Harley Butte, and not himself, who understands the power and influence of true creativity. Harry realizes through music and the efforts of Harley Butte to achieve a level of perfection that violence is ultimately an unsuccessful means to an end. Hannah redeems Harry by making it clear that he will dedicate his life to constructive, not destructive, behavior; although he cannot create music as beautiful as Butte's, Harry commits himself to discovering the musical potential within language. The beauty of Harley's music exorcises the violence of Harry's actions against Peter and grants him the opportunity for a fresh beginning.

Nightwatchmen: Experiments with Perspective

Harriman and Prissy Monroe also appear in Hannah's second novel, *Nightwatchmen* (1973), but the primary character is a dissatisfied, effeminate Southern loner named Thorpe Trove who spends his substantial inheritance on a 14-room estate near the fictional Southwestern Mississippi University in Pass Christian. Whereas *Geronimo Rex* explores Harry's progression toward manhood through events that indicate a maturity of thought and an ability to overcome interest in the self, *Nightwatchmen* traces Trove's circular movement from self-imposed exile to humanitarian to exile again. In *Rex,* Harry's interior monologue and his series of discrete, episodic adventures tie the disparate incidents of the novel together; his random, violent thoughts and actions drive the narrative toward a unity derived more from the consistency of the protagonist's thoughts than the complexity of plot. *Nightwatchmen,* on the other hand, achieves unity through its adherence to plot elements designed to resemble and satirize clues from a murder mystery. The reader is driven to finish the novel, not only because of interest in the future of the protagonist, but just as importantly, to discover the identity of the killer who is decapitating the nightwatchmen in Old Main, the English building on the Southwestern Mississippi University campus.

Hannah told Jan Gretland that *Nightwatchmen* is his "most deliberately Gothic book," and he believes much of its failure stems from his overreliance on a complicated narrative: "The more contrived a book I try to write, the more plot I put in, the worse I become as a writer" (Gretland, 234). And, indeed, much of the novel advances through a series of broadly comic and unlikely plot devices, from mistaken identities to sentimental criminals, from all-destructive hurricanes to mass infatuations.

Critics who lauded *Geronimo Rex* found Hannah's second novel disappointing, in spite of its experimental form, and it was largely ignored. Jonathan Yardley of the *New York Review of Books* wrote that the novel "sustains so little narrative interest that its unastonishing conclusions are scarcely worth the labor of reaching them,"[9] and Arnold Asrelsky of *Library Journal* believed that "too often the narrative drags, burdened by the interspersed diffuse monologues which often strain for wit or cuteness."[10] John Skow

called *Nightwatchmen* a "perverse and disappointing mistake"; he felt that
the "nervous, jerky mood of the new novel" prevented Hannah from experi-
menting successfully with language as in *Geronimo Rex*.[11] Many critics
agreed that the novel seemed hurriedly written, perhaps as a quick fol-
low-up to the success of *Geronimo Rex*, and Hannah admits that he wrote
the novel while teaching a full courseload. But a closer look at *Nightwatchmen* not only indicates thematic similarities to *Rex*, but reveals the basis for
much of the experimentation in Hannah's later fiction.

The central character in the novel is Thorpe Trove, whose parents were
slain on their second honeymoon in 1944. After his guardian aunt dies, he
buys a house with his inheritance and, to circumvent his increasing loneliness and reliance on alcohol, decides to take in boarders. Most are from the
English department at Old Main. Harriman Monroe and his wife Prissy
come first, followed by an assortment of eccentrics and academics: the pretentious Englishman Anthony Weymouth, the black Magee, and the non-
descript Bob Hill, Hallman Bryant, and Charles Israel. When a mysterious
stranger humorously called the "knocker" begins striking academic "bores"
on the back of the head at the university and knocking them out (much to
everyone's delight), Trove starts to compile taped transcriptions to discover
the assailant's identity. But after two nightwatchmen are brutally slaughtered (one by decapitation), Trove suspects that the case is more complicated than he originally assumed: the "knocker" and the "killer" may not be
the same person.

Hannah divides *Nightwatchmen* into 15 chapters, 9 recounting the
taped transcripts of interviews conducted by Trove. Each subject taped by
Trove advances the murder plot while describing the relationships that
graduate students and professors at Southwestern Mississippi share with
the boarders in Pass Christian. This structure enables Hannah to emphasize the irony implicit in multiperspectivism—each character offers a different version of the "truth" and each version reveals much about the
characters being interviewed. Conducted in 1969, each of the first four
interviews—"William Tell," "Lawrence Head," "Harriman Monroe," and
"Didi Sweet"—reveals information garnered from Trove's taping sessions
by recounting the same tale. Not until readers explore all four perspectives
do they discover all of the facts beneath the layers of self-deception. So although Hannah abandons his use of characters as foils to define a single
protagonist in *Nightwatchmen*, he still relies on a variety of perspectives to
narrate the "truth."

Such a structure allows Hannah to replay incidents almost cinematically
to provide four very different scenarios of one evening. Tell, for example,

frightens fellow graduate student Didi Sweet in order to make sexual advances, while Head, jealous of Tell's apparent success with Didi, terrifies the two hoping to abort their potential lovemaking. Harry, who prefers Didi to his own wife Prissy, forms an alliance with Head to disrupt the ensuing relationship between Didi and Tell, and Didi, in her taped transcript, explains in detail her relationship with all three men. Ultimately, the reader is left to determine the truth from the collective stories.

Between the nine chapters of taped transcripts running from 1969 to 1971, Hannah inserts six chapters entitled "Thorpe Trove" (or "T.T."). Written in first-person narration, these chapters smooth the transitions between transcripts and focus the novel on Trove's eventual escape (albeit temporary and incomplete) from his self-imposed exile. The "transcribed" chapters loosely resemble the variety of perspectives explored in William Faulkner's *As I Lay Dying,* and represent Hannah's attempt to break from the traditional structure of the mystery, not only to satirize its form, but also to heighten the mystery that lies within subjective response.

In the *Dictionary of Literary Biography,* Charles Israel describes the rich and complex texture of *Nightwatchmen:* "Hannah's successful experiment with minor narrators speaking through the tape transcriptions allows the development of a complex texture, offering a telling counterpoint to Thorpe's sad and comic story."[12] Some critics, such as Donald R. Noble, complain that the similarity of voices in *Nightwatchmen* ultimately defeats the individuality of perspective: "The problem here for Hannah, in abandoning first person, is that Hannah's 'voice' intrudes everywhere and the various characters tend to sound alike. . . . Multiple point of view is not to be Hannah's forte" (Noble, 41). But Hannah is not striving for individuality through multiperspectivism. He is primarily interested in discovering the humor and irony implicit in perspectives whose similarity depends on sharing the language and identity of professions; in other words, rather than create a plethora of individual voices like Faulkner in *As I Lay Dying,* Hannah originates three distinct categories of voices in *Nightwatchmen,* each influenced by job and social status and each defined by a specific type of violent action.

The first group represents the abstruse and pretentious academic perspective, characterized by circular argument, dense logic, and abstract thought, probably parodying the academic life of which Hannah was then a part. Paralyzed by an overzealous emphasis on critical analysis, academics such as William Tell, Lawrence Head, and Harriman Monroe rely more heavily on abstract thought than on direct action. When Tell, for example, frightens himself in Old Main, he praises the depth of thought that allows

him the freedom to daydream: "I congratulated myself on the degree of ab-
straction I had flung myself into. The fiend might have come in the door,
and here I would have been, the statue of an absorbed scholar—my eyes
and heart, my body and mind with Calypso and the sorrowfully fornicating
Odysseus."[13] For Head, even urinating inspires a level of personal fantasy
and imagination: "I was propulsed by my own water to the surface of another planet, where I saw women petting tigers on the steps of an old tem-
ple overgrown with creepers and overhung with leaves of the banana plant"
(*NW*, 52). And Harriman Monroe, still obsessed with violence, reacts more
slowly than he did in *Geronimo Rex* because of an academically imposed
need to analyze a situation before acting upon it: "I had come to some pla-
teau of decisions, a broiling plain, but at least it was a plain, over which
hung two dominant clouds wherein there was a directive; on the right: kick
Ned's face; on the left: suffer all men, your brothers—" (*NW*, 63).

The nature of violence in *Nightwatchmen*, therefore, differs from that in
Geronimo Rex, especially with the group of academics. Like Harriman
Monroe of *Rex*, they still resort to violent action for self-gratification, but
their actions are less spontaneous, more calculated. Hannah contrasts their
petty, violent machinations to earn sexual and academic favors with the
more desperate violence of the second group, the blue-collar workers.

Two characters in *Nightwatchmen*, Frank Theron Knockre, a security
guard and plumber, and Douglas David Lotrieux, a projectionist who eventually reveals himself as the "knocker," illustrate Hannah's experimentation
with language to contrast the academic perspective with that of the blue-
collar worker. Unlike Tell, Head, or Monroe, Knockre and Lotrieux not
only act spontaneously without the deterrent of abstract thought, but also
resent the academics for their inability to transmute the conclusions they
reach into some form of physical action. Knockre dislikes the worthlessness
and indecisiveness of the university professors enough to feel satisfaction
with the violence taken against them: "It wasn't no affair of mine about the
professors and students being knocked out before that, though I known of
it. To put it on the line, I was privately amused at it. . . . None of them on
the campus knew shit from Shinola" (*NW*, 112). Lotrieux, who likes to
imagine himself as "La Enigma," tries to bridge the gap between himself
and the academics by bopping them on the head, ironically eliminating any
chance of future communication: "There was the back of the heads, that is
all they'd give me. Or a flick of the eyes, and then their heads bending
down again at their books. . . . I was looking for faces but all I got was a
flick of the eyes and the back of their heads" (*NW*, 148). Because neither
Knockre nor Lotrieux knows how to communicate with the graduate stu-

dents, the back of the head is literally the closest either comes to sharing thoughts or discussing ideas.

Both Knockre and Lotrieux use concrete images and specific, clear language to inform Trove of their inability to communicate with graduate students. Knockre and Lotrieux's men's club, arranged not around any particular common interest or mutual respect, meets in a projection booth Monday through Thursday nights simply to discuss with other nonacademics confusing current events or to confess embarrassing personal failures. Although their reliance on violence is more base and natural than the forced violence of the academics, the nightwatchmen still find the threat of real danger abhorrent and frightening. When two members of this group, Conrad and Spell, are brutally killed in Old Main, their friends in the men's club long for vengeance but lack the strength to pursue the killer. Hannah strongly suggests that a member of this group is responsible for the deaths in Old Main, but, ultimately, Knockre and Lotrieux only discover information that will lead Trove and detective Howard Hunter to discover the real murderer, Ralph White.

The first-person perspectives of Thorpe Trove and Didi Sweet and the third-person narration of Howard Hunter form the third triumvirate in *Nightwatchmen*. These characters represent the possibility of balancing abstract thought with practical action. Whereas the academics often think themselves out of acting and the nightwatchmen act without thought, Trove, Sweet, and Hunter sense inadequacies in their lives and act thoughtfully, emotionally, and sometimes illogically to overcome them. Trove becomes a landlord to prevent what seems an inevitable drive toward total isolation; Sweet embraces Southern romanticism to find a worthy companion; and Hunter pursues the accidental death of the man assumed to be the killer more to form friendships than to solve the crime itself. Although none of the three successfully reaches his or her goal, each comes closer to finding personal satisfaction than anyone else in the novel.

Ironically, it is through their union that the three profit most. Trove's borders temporarily alleviate his loneliness, but when Hurricane Camille decimates his house and leaves him nearly destitute, he buys a trailer in the hope of retaining some sense of the community he has fostered. After he is ultimately used and deserted by graduate students such as Harry Monroe, he finds solace and satisfaction in Didi's arms: "All I say is bless God for the man-woman relationship. Bless Didi for being so full of sighs and laughter during the night. Thank God for the enduring strength of Nature that I was no disappointment in our orgy" (*NW,* 155). And although their relationship ultimately fails, Didi still looks to Trove years later for answers to her question of loneliness: "Will you tell me why I can only love in pieces? I can never get my head, my heart, and my body into it all together? I want one long evening on the beach alone with you" (*NW,* 188). The object of affection of every male in Pass Christian and at Southwestern Mississippi University, Didi chooses Trove, not the academics, to fulfill her mission of finding a Southern gentleman, "some man who had etiquette right from the heart and the time to love without anything immediately to gain. Hold you without almost touching you till you had time to fill up with love like a peach ready to bust. Take you out in a grove with a picnic basket his mother fixed for you" (*NW,* 88). Trove fulfills for Didi, at least temporarily, this image of the genteel Southern gentleman while she builds for him his self-esteem. Theirs is a mutually beneficial relationship, and although Didi leaves Trove after he proposes marriage and children, neither is happy without the other.

After Didi's desertion, Howard Hunter helps to give Trove's life meaning again. The detective who points out that Trove and the graduate students, in their overzealous search for Ralph White, have shot the wrong man, reinterests Trove first in the murder case and then in life. Financially distressed, Trove takes a job at K-Mart selling shoes and catches mononucleosis. Although they are not yet friends, Hunter takes care of Trove: "Howard came over to the trailer daily. He thought I had one foot in the grave and I wasn't so sure I didn't myself. I was bowled over by a raging worthlessness in my throat, my eyes, my brain, and my bowels. Howard cooked for me from the cans in the pantry. Then he'd watch TV with me. I didn't have the strength to hold the cards" (*NW,* 216). After his eventual recovery, Trove stages a reunion between himself, his boarders, and Didi, only to find himself the outsider again. Hunter realizes that the former graduate students have abused Trove and that Didi has caused him grief a second time: "I'll bet they all *said* a lot, didn't they? I'll bet they're the type that don't know who the hell they are or what they're doing so they just go around jabbering to prove they're at least a noise somewhere. I know the type" (*NW,* 220). Hunter senses the inadequacies in the academics' penchant for discussion rather than action; Hunter's friendship, in which giving is just as significant as taking and concrete action is more important than abstract philosophizing, actually redeems Trove at the end of the novel by making him realize that a simple gesture of kindness is superior to a vague discussion of virtue.

Within this third group, then, both Sweet and Hunter contribute to Trove's eventual return to mankind by encouraging within him an understanding of true humanity and the need for action to accompany philosophy. By the end of the novel Trove has developed into a more satisfied, less ostentatious version of Harriman Monroe in *Geronimo Rex,* one who finds pleasure in a simple game of cards or a conversation with a friend.

The violence Hannah associates with Trove is less destructive than Monroe's in *Geronimo Rex;* in fact, Sweet, Trove, and Hunter are all associated more with the unnecessary violence in the novel, not the grotesque and exaggerated violence of the young Harry or the disturbed Peter Lepoyster. Noble points out that "*Nightwatchmen* ends in chaos, natural and man-made, with Hurricane Camille roaring through to kill off some of the participants and level the terrain entirely, bringing everyone out into the open physically and emotionally" (Noble, 41). Hannah parallels the violence of Hurricane Camille with the discoveries of Trove, Sweet, and Hunter; each understands that change is achieved only when the layers of self-deception are stripped away not only by the hurricane, but also by their eventual dissatisfaction with their lifestyles and the inactivity of those around them. Didi threatens to leave her husband when he worships her too completely; she understands finally that obsessive love is less fulfilling than finding a balanced affection derived from mutual respect rather than desperate need. Hunter and Trove find themselves together at the end of *Nightwatchmen.* Hunter nourishes the sick Trove with soup and games of cards, and Trove realizes his strong affection for the "rampant and smug" Hunter:

I broke out of my death state a few nights later when I was dealt three kings, including my favorite fellow. I woke up betting. There seemed to be everything to live for.

"What you got?" asked Howard.

His spectacles were on fire with hope for me and him (*NW,* 232).

Trove finds personal salvation in *Nightwatchmen,* not by solving a mystery, capturing the essence of people on taped transcripts, or resorting to violence; rather, he discovers hope for the future through friendship and company, reminiscent of Harry and Lariat's mutual appreciation for music at the end of *Geronimo Rex.*

Nightwatchmen is ultimately, like *Rex,* a novel about the miracle of communication. Whereas *Rex* ends with Monroe and his professor realizing the communicative power of music, *Nightwatchmen* concludes with a simple act of humanity every bit as powerful and beautiful as the music that Harley Butte creates. Although Hannah's experimentation with perspective in *Nightwatchmen* lacks the strength and humor of his language in *Rex,* he does explore with finesse and insight the irony implicit in the lack of communication that often accompanies a higher education. In spite of their disparate backgrounds, the academics, the blue-collar workers, and the humanitarians share a need similar to Whitfield Peter's, Harley Butte's, and Harriman Monroe's in *Geronimo Rex:* the need for compassion and a common basis for communication, be it music, conversation, or a game of cards.

Donald R. Noble points out that much of the significance of *Nightwatchmen* lies in its title: "Hannah seems to be saying, we are all nightwatchmen. We all stand lonely watches and are hungry for communication and friends" (Noble, 42). The lonely vigils experienced by the security guards in the Old Main are shared by almost everyone in the novel: Didi Sweet, who waits patiently for a man who will treat her with respect; Lawrence Head, who looks for a companion with whom to share ideas; David Lotrieux, who knocks people over the head rather than risk alienation; and Harriman Monroe, who realizes that his heart "is a piece of false junk" (*NW,* 68). Violence toward others brings only a temporary solution to the problems of the characters in *Geronimo Rex* and *Nightwatchmen.* Ultimately, Hannah's characters violently reexamine the self to discover that the true possibility of salvation lies within man's latent and untapped ability to create new avenues for communication.

Chapter Two
"Crucified by Truth": Narrative Voices in *Airships*

In "Water Liars," the first story in Hannah's collection *Airships* (1978), the narrator and his wife share stories of past sexual liaisons during a drunken, late-night truth session: "I had a mildly exciting and usual history, and she had about the same, which surprised me. For ten years she'd sworn I was the first. I could not believe her history was exactly equal with mine. It hurt me to think that in an era when there were supposed to be virgins she had allowed anyone but *me*, and so on."[1] To escape the truth about his wife, the narrator vacations at Farte Cove (pronounced "Far-tay") where elderly fishing chums regularly swap tall tales about sexual relations with ghostly apparitions, fish the size of puppies pulled from the river without bait, and a "good hunnerd" high school students discovered smoking dope and swimming naked. When a new, younger man, "maybe sixty," recounts interrupting his daughter Charlotte's affair with an older, mustached gentleman hidden off the cove of the Yazoo River, he shocks and alienates the group of fisherman. Accustomed only to exaggerated accounts of supernatural feats, the tall-tale spinners demand that he take his true story elsewhere. The narrator, empathizing with the implications of the new man's story, invites him to his cabin. At the end of "Water Liars," the narrator and the outcast storyteller fish silently together, kindred spirits "both crucified by truth" (*A*, 7).

The inability to face "truth" about themselves and those around them is the characteristic that binds together most of the narrators in Hannah's 20 stories entitled *Airships*. In his interview with R. Vanarsdall, Hannah admitted that the reality of the moment in "Water Liars" is what his character cannot face: "and then the reality of this old guy he meets there and his daughter: it's really kind of a growing-up thing, and this is really what happens. You don't meet the ghost of Yazoo out there; it's your own daughter getting fucked by some guy with a mustache that you don't even know. . . . It's the real shocker. The young man's dealing with it in his wife's story too" (Vanarsdall, 332). Like Harriman Monroe and Thorpe Trove of *Geronimo Rex* and *Nightwatchmen*, respectively, the narrators in *Airships* look for both intellectual and emotional truth, but unlike the protagonists of Hannah's first two novels, most of the characters in *Airships* are despicable, lonely, wounded people unable to act without relying on the comforting falsehoods they must create to survive. In "Outrage and Speculation: Barry Hannah's *Airships*," Allen Shepherd writes that the stories' "narrators are commonly of the walking wounded or disabled variety, literally or metaphorically battered veterans,"[2] and Donald R. Noble believes that in *Airships*, "Hannah creates a desperate, pathetic world . . . a world in which the characters are on edge, wounded by love but still seeking love as the cure" (Noble, 43). The protagonists in the short stories consistently experience physical, mental, and/or emotional pain, and they remain unable to reverse the destructive patterns they themselves have created.

In *Geronimo Rex* and *Nightwatchmen* Hannah concentrates as much on characters in the process of wounding others as he does on those who are defeated by life. For every Thorpe Trove, overcome by circumstance, there exists a Harriman Monroe or a Lawrence Head, overcoming circumstances through violent action. In *Airships* Hannah emphasizes the Thorpe Troves, characters bewildered and defeated who find themselves unable to understand or deal with the hurt inflicted on them by others.

In "Love Too Long," for example, a narrator similar to the husband in "Water Liars" literally believes that he will "die from love" after his wife, whom he both adores and fears, divorces him a second time; in "Knowing He Was Not My Kind Yet I Followed" Confederate corporal Deed Ainsworth pursues an unrequited and unpromising homosexual love for Jeb Stuart; in "Our Secret Home" an academic and his wife conclude that their friends have deserted them because of the husband's feebleminded twin sister, with whom he may be having an incestuous relationship; and in "Testimony of Pilot" the narrator vows never again to tell or write another story after his talented musician friend Quadberry is killed in Vietnam. These narrators, and indeed most of the characters in *Airships,* find lying to be the most convenient survival tactic. Bending the truth allows them to avoid facing the possibility of permanent isolation while it also offers the faint hope of personal and domestic redemption. But unlike Thorpe Trove, who finds at the end of *Nightwatchmen* that friendship offers the possibility of grace, the characters created by Hannah in *Airships* are left without even the means to communicate with others. They all resemble the husband in "Water Liars," whose thirty-third birthday reminds him of Christ's crucifixion: "Last year I turned thirty-three years old and, raised a Baptist, I had a sense of being Jesus and coming to something decided in my life—because we all know Jesus was crucified at thirty-three" (*A,* 3). Neither the husband nor most of the narrators discover this "something decided," because achieving truth through honest communication is a cross too difficult for them to bear. For Hannah's characters, lying may be ultimately unsatisfying and destructive, but it is easier and more immediately gratifying than facing truth. The real irony in the Christ parallel is that, although the narrators in *Airships* create and accept their own crucifixions, their lives are devoid of significance and thus their suffering usually affects no one but themselves.

These narrators and their similar situations help to bind the collection of short stories together, making them a unified whole. In "Everything that Rises" Michael Malone points out that Hannah's *Airships* is most reminiscent of Faulkner's *Go Down Moses:* "In an ultimate, though not obvious way, Hannah's stories are fused together thematically. . . . Individually, they are beautifully built, but the construction work is so organic that he didn't have to leave the braces showing."[3] Hannah ties the collection together not through an alliance or overemphasis of similar place or time; as Malone suggests, he overcomes regional ties to forge thematic and stylistic ones. His characters share common misfortune, and most accept and/or attack pain in a similarly unsuccessful manner. He writes primarily about the South, from Biloxi, Slidell, and Mobile to Richmond, Atlanta, and Tuscaloosa, and Hannah's consistent first-person narrative style creates a unified chorus of misfortune and regret. While the dialect and sensibility of the characters is southern, the connection between them does not depend on background and place; instead, Hannah's narrators share an inability to overcome their limited perspectives. Blinded by emotion, Hannah's characters act rashly, often resorting to violence to achieve immediate results. Through first-person narration, Hannah delves into their psyches, presenting their viewpoints straightforwardly while focusing upon the irony of their self-created dilemmas. In other words, he balances first-person perspective with an implied authorial position, illustrating the depth and complexity of behavioral responses that inspire action and initiate violence.

Most critics reacted favorably to *Airships.* The collection was the first winner of the Arnold Gingrich Short Fiction Award and also earned an Award for Literature from the American Academy and Institute of Arts and Letters. George M. Kelly wrote in *Library Journal* that Hannah "is a brutal and savage writer, but worth enduring because of his humor, his poetic metaphors, and his well worked-out symbols,"[4] and Michael Wood believed that *Airships* represents for Hannah a move past the voice of the South: "There is a kinship with Eudora Welty, perhaps, or Flannery O'Connor—an eccentric response to a world of fading but rigid social convention—but Mr. Hannah's style is more abrupt. His South is more scattered, too, and seems finally to represent an America that is to be found East, North, and West as well, a disheveled modern country caught between Shiloh and Vietnam."[5] And although Robert Towers wrote harshly in the *New York Review of Books* of Hannah's excessive violence and inconsistent tone, he admitted that "several scenes are so beautifully mounted and sustained that they briefly (too briefly) exalt his artistry to the level we associate with Eudora Welty and Flannery O'Connor."[6]

Like O'Connor, Hannah manipulates circumstance to surprise and even alienate the reader, and like Welty, he often creates a disinterested but amused authorial persona to comment objectively upon the characters and their hypocrisies. But the originality of Hannah's vision in *Airships* lies in his inventive use of language to describe three distinct types of battle-grounds, each indicative of a specific type of human behavior. The first is a literal battlefield, that of the Civil and Vietnam wars. Hannah juxtaposes stories about both wars until the distinction between the two becomes pur-posely blurred. These intentional parallels suggest that man's emotional and physical reactions to the stress associated with warfare have remained essentially unchanged over the last 100 years. The second type of battle-ground is domestic, which Hannah uses to introduce emotional and intel-lectual conflicts between the home and the heart. The third and most abstract battlefield is internal, in which the rules of warfare are personal, symbolic, and obscure. Although categorizing stories often risks trivializing the breadth and scope of a collection, such distinctions are useful in discuss-ing *Airships,* not only to analyze the focus of the work, but also to illustrate Hannah's progression as a stylist, his experiments with language, and his unifying thematic principles.

The Literal Battlefield

Although Hannah's use of violence is often a point of controversy among critics, his stories set in times of actual war are surprisingly personal and subtle. "Testimony of Pilot," the first story in the collection that explores the consequences of the Vietnam War, focuses upon the narrator, Williams, and his friendship with and growing respect for Quadberry, whom he nick-names Arden or Ard. The story begins by describing Williams, between 10 and 12 years old, shooting M-80 explosives from cannons with his friend Radcleve. Like Harriman Monroe, Williams finds this violent means of ex-pression his only real effort at communication, and it humorously intro-duces the narrator to young Quadberry, saxophone player and unintentional victim of the M-80's wrath. Quadberry, like Harley Butte in *Geronimo Rex,* communicates through music more effectively than the narrator, who plays the drum: "When he played, I heard the sweetness. I heard the horn which finally brought human *talk* into the realm of music" (*A*, 24). When their high school band director is accidentally killed before a concert, Ard exhibits his leadership qualities by triumphantly directing the band, resulting in the maturation of the entire company: "Boys became men and girls became women as Quadberry directed us through *Bolero*" (*A*, 28). Williams feels so inferior to Ard, in fact, that Hannah does not even introduce the narrator's name until the story is moving toward its conclusion.

Ard not only exhibits musical talent and a penchant for leadership, but he also attracts the attention of Lilian, Clinton's most desirable majorette (with whom Williams is, of course, infatuated). While Williams attends college, at which his drum playing eventually causes a complete loss of hearing, Quadberry abandons music and Lilian to fly jets off of the *Bonhomme Richard*, an aircraft carrier headed for Vietnam. As Quadberry successfully dedicates himself with unqualified zeal to his profession as a pilot, Williams takes a job as a lead writer in an advertising firm and makes unsuccessful advances toward Lilian.

Hannah emphasizes Williams's jealous recognition of Ard's ability to transfer his affection from music to flight: "Two of his mates were taken down by these missiles. But Quadberry, as on saxophone, had endless learned techniques. He'd put his jets perpendicular in the air and made the SAMs look silly" (*A*, 40). But Vietnam ultimately betrays even Quadberry, and in turn, Williams. Ard returns home with severe neck and spine injuries that prevent him from flying and playing the sax. To ease the pain from the war injury, Quadberry undergoes experimental surgery, and although the chances are 75 percent in his favor, he dies on the operating table, leaving Williams devastated:

"Quadberry lost his gamble at Emory Hospital in Atlanta. The brilliant surgeon his age lost him. Quadberry died. He died with his Arabian nose in the air."

"That is why I told this story and will never tell another." (*A*, 44)

Ard's death, then, becomes Williams's impetus for telling the story, and ironically, also the reason that he will never further the communication refined throughout his friendship with the saxophone player.

In "Testimony of Pilot" Hannah illustrates many of the themes and techniques present in the Civil War and Vietnam stories of *Airships*. He presents a narrator, ineffectual at communication, who lives vicariously through the successful communicative ability of another. The war in "Testimony of Pilot" serves as a catalyst altering the course of fate previously determined by Quadberry himself. As Allen Shepherd writes, "Vietnam is clearly on Hannah's mind, with deranged, doomed Quadberry as one of the best and the brightest" (70). War's primary destructive power, then, exists not in its extrinsic threat to life, but in its ability to block previous avenues of communication, forcing characters to search for new ones. Williams meets this challenge through his need to recount Quadberry's story. But ironically, although in the tale he achieves real communication for the first time, he will not tell another tale. The tragedy of Quadberry's death and the loss Williams experiences paradoxically both fosters and destroys his potential as a writer and storyteller. Vietnam leaves Quadberry dead and Williams defeated and incommunicative.

In "Midnight and I'm Not Famous Yet," the second Vietnam story in *Airships*, Hannah describes a narrator, like Williams, who lives vicariously through the abilities of another. Bobby Smith is a soldier who is partially responsible for the capture and death of a North Vietnamese general, Li Dap. In the midst of battle, Smith is reunited with photographer and homeboy Ike "Tubby" Wooten from Redwood, whose pictures express the grace and ability of celebrity golfer John Whitelaw: "But the thing that got me was that John Whitelaw *cared* so much about what he was doing. It made me love America to know he was in it, and I hadn't loved anything for nigh three years then" (*A*, 108). Like Quadberry in "Testimony of Pilot," Whitelaw in "Midnight and I'm Not Famous Yet" represents the narrator's ideal combination of manhood, artistic sensibility, and successful communication: "The way John Whitelaw looked, it sort of rebuked yourself ever hoping to call yourself a man" (*A*, 108). In fact, Tubby, Whitelaw, and captured North Vietnamese general Li Dap all offer a combined artistic heroic sensibility that the narrator finds lacking in himself. At the end of the story, with Tubby and Li Dap casualties of war, Bobby is left a displaced retired lieutenant, unable to procure Tubby's pictures from the Pentagon or to encourage the artistic potential within himself.

But unlike Williams in "Testimony of Pilot," Bobby at least illustrates some possibility of change inspired by Whitelaw and his own time spent in Vietnam. In the war he is successful because of his uncanny ability to slaughter the enemy: "I'd killed so many gooks. I'd killed them with machine guns, mortars, howitzers, knives, wire, me and my boys" (*A*, 113). But Tubby's pictures of John Whitelaw make Bobby realize that his life "had gone straight from teenage giggling to horror" (*A*, 114); he can no longer appreciate the violence within himself. Beauty he finds only in the "wonderful and peaceful" art of golf rather than in combat with the potential of real danger. At the end of the story, for example, Bobby reverently attends a John Whitelaw–Whitney Maxwell golf tournament. When Whitelaw loses the match and the crowd reacts despondently, only Bobby realizes that the wonder of golf lies in its nonaggressive definition of victory and defeat: "Fools! Fools! I thought. Love it! Love the loss as well as the gain. Go home and dig it. Nobody was killed. We saw victory and defeat, and they were both wonderful" (*A,* 118). Vietnam had left Bobby just a "killer of gooks," but Whitelaw and golf bring the realization that sometimes *observing* is more gratifying than *initiating* action. For Bobby, real beauty, after Vietnam, lies not in the physical violence of warfare but within the nondestructive competitiveness of the golf pro.

Ironically, Hannah uses the captured North Vietnamese general Li Dap in "Midnight" to point to parallels between the Civil War and Vietnam. Not only does the general know and admire the strategies of Robert E. Lee and Jeb Stuart, but he believes his side will win in Vietnam because of precedents set during the Civil War: "It's relative to your war in the nineteenth century. The South had slavery. The North must purge it so that it is a healthy region of our country" (*A,* 113). Michael Malone points out that Faulkner territory serves as the setting for the Civil War stories: "The battleground for Hannah's fight is in Faulkner's territory, in the character of the Confederate General, Jeb Stuart, who figures centrally in four of the twenty stories, and always ambivalently, both as glorious hero and murdering fool" (Malone, 706). With Stuart, Hannah presents a paradoxical figure. On the one hand, the famous general exhibits a sensitivity to delicate situations and an ability to communicate effectively; on the other hand, he illustrates the insensitivity and blind prejudice necessary to achieve success in the midst of warfare. Ultimately, he symbolizes for the vainglorious South an almost comic mixture of foolishness, humor, and noble intentions.

In one of the best of the Jeb Stuart stories in *Airships,* "Knowing He Was Not My Kind Yet I Followed," Hannah traces the admiration of homosexual Corporal Deed Ainsworth for Jeb Stuart. Unlike Smith or Williams, Ainsworth loves foraging for food and loot but hates "this murdering business that goes along with it" (*A,* 143). Because Ainsworth is a "nancy" none of the men in his Confederate outfit will allow him to share conversation, so he remains alone with his thoughts. His admiration for Stuart grows as he realizes that only the general continues to believe in the Confederate cause: "There is nobody who does not believe in Jeb Stuart. Oh, the zany, purposeful eyes, the haggard gleam, the feet of his lean horse high in the air, his rotting flannel shirt under the old soiled grays, and his heroic body odor! He makes one want to be a Christian" (*A,* 145). In an encounter with Stuart, Ainsworth learns that Stuart accepts and respects men for who they are, independent of sexual tendencies: "Because the Creator made you strange, my man. . . . God made us different and we should love His differences as well as His likenesses" (*A*, 146). And even though Stuart chides the black minstrel George for calling Ainsworth a "nancy," he regards the banjo player as a brother and embraces him, piquing Ainsworth's jealousy.

At the end of the story, when Ainsworth is being attacked by a Yank with a fork, he threatens Stuart as the general attempts to rescue him. Ainsworth's hatred of manslaughter results in his eventual capture and imprisonment in Albany, where he hears of Stuart's death: "They'd killed Jeb in Virginia. I don't think there's much reservoir of self left to me now. The earth will never see his kind again" (*A*, 148). The sense of comic despair Ainsworth illustrates at the end of the story reflects Hannah's own feelings about Stuart: "Stuart was better [than Robert E. Lee] because he liked music and he was capable of being a fool. He failed gravely at Gettysburg; he wasn't in the right place. . . . He was up there riding for glory. . . . That's the kind of asshole soldier I would be, I fear. There's a weakness in Stuart that makes him more likely for fiction" (Vanarsdall, 330). Ainsworth's adulation of Stuart emphasizes the romantic glory of the Southern legend: "I have seen it many times, but there is no glory like Jeb Stuart putting spurs in his sorrel and escaping the Minie balls" (*A*, 148). But Hannah, although he respects Stuart's dedication and nobility, laughs at Stuart as well. In Ainsworth's encounter with Stuart in the text, Hannah describes a general who hides the defeat at Gettysburg from his men, who writes in the same letter to his wife about the inalienable right of the Confederacy and "the memory of [her] hot hairy jumping nexus" (*A*, 146), who suggests that the Lord has no more room "for another nigger's thoughts" (*A*, 147). Like the tall tales told by the men off Farte Cove in "Water Liars," Stuart purposely creates a heroic image of himself. That Ainsworth falls for this self-made legend only illustrates the corporal's susceptibility to myth and physical grace; Hannah makes certain his readers are not so gullible.

In "Dragged Fighting from the Tomb" Hannah creates another Stuart myth, this one fictitiously chronicling the general's death. When asked by Vanarsdall if he was trying to kill off Jeb Stuart in the story literally to exorcise the character from his future fiction, Hannah replied, "I wasn't trying to get rid of Jeb Stuart and he didn't go that way, of course. He was shot at Yellow Tavern. . . . I was trying to stay consistent with the character of young Captain Howard to old Captain Howard" (Vanarsdall, 329). In "Knowing He Was Not My Kind Yet I Followed" Ainsworth takes pleasure in creating fantasies about Stuart; the romantic image of the noble warrior on his steed sustains the corporal, and he relies on this fantasy to justify the violence of the Civil War. In "Dragged Fighting from the Tomb" Captain Howard, murderer of Stuart, fights instead to discover truth, not romantic fantasy. He holds an old Yankee prisoner, promising him freedom in exchange for "the most exquisite truths he knows" (A, 51). When he receives a string of beliefs rather than absolute truths, he asks questions inspired by Darwin's theory of the origin of the species (published four years before the time of this story, 1863): "Where is the angry machine of all of us? Why is God such a blurred magician? Why are you begging for your life if you believe those things? Prove to me that you're better than the rabbits we ate last night" (A, 51). Because the Yankee is unable or unwilling to answer, Howard ambushes the old man's camp and kills four soldiers. To Howard, love of violence is justifiable in a world without one single, important truth.

In fact, Captain Howard places more value on his horse's life than he does on his own or those of other soldiers. He expresses the philosophy "*that a good animal knows his man*," and proves it by ordering his obedient steed, Mount Auburn, to fall down, prance, or even kill on command (A, 52). When Auburn is shot, Howard destroys the entire city and is congratulated by an envious Jeb Stuart, who advises Howard to mourn more for people than for animals (A, 58). Jailed by Stuart for insubordination over this advice (Howard reacts violently to any slight made against his horse), Howard escapes across the Mason-Dixon line in the enemy's outfit and murders Stuart:

"I shot him right in the brow, so that not another thought would pass about me or about himself or about the South, before death. I knew I was killing a man with wife and children."

"I never looked at what the body did on its big horse." (A, 58)

Loyalty to his murdered horse drives Howard to kill the legendary general, making Howard a legend himself 37 years later (1900) at a convention of Confederate veterans. Accused there of killing Jeb Stuart, Howard leaves the convention to seek refuge with Mount Auburn's grandchild, a horse never given a name: "I suppose I was waiting for him to say what he wanted, to talk. But Christ is his name, this muscle and heart striding under me" (A, 60). Howard, ironically, feels comfortable only with animals over whom he can exert his control; he abandons mankind to seek peace and refuge in the company of horses.

Like the other protagonists in the war stories in *Airships*, Howard is left without truth or human contact. His search leads only to violence without reason and civilian life without peace. Although he destroys the regiment,

Howard spares the life of the old man who cannot tell him one single truth. Hannah admitted to Vanarsdall that he uses violence here primarily to promote truth: "I like the kind of violence that provokes the conversation that Howard has with that Union old man, that when your body gets threatened, your mind tightens up. You lie less when things are against the wall, and things that are really meaningful come forth" (Vanarsdall, 324–25). For example, when he asks the Yankee to tell him *something, something wise,* the old man replies, "There is no wisdom, Johnny Reb. . . . There's only tomorrow, if you're lucky. Don't kill us. Let us have tomorrow" (*A,* 57). Existence for those in the Civil and the Vietnam wars, according to Hannah in *Airships,* is without purpose, meaning, or truth. Hannah said to Jan Gretland that both wars defeated the American public because of the extent of the loss involved: "The Vietnam War was a big subject in my youth. I didn't go. It was shocking for America to lose, and it took some terrific readjustments to get used to the fact. Maybe [Walker] Percy was talking about the way losing the Civil War made you a spiritual outlander. Maybe what he meant was that defeat made you eloquent, more eloquent than victory. And I write about defeated people often" (Gretland, 235). Williams, Smith, Ainsworth, and Howard are all spiritual outlanders and casualties of war. They survive, but are left without the ability to communicate their pain or find comfort to ease their losses. Their stories, as recounted by Hannah, represent their final and unsuccessful efforts at communication.

The Domestic Battlefield

The second type of warfare that Hannah explores in *Airships* occurs on the domestic front. The physical violence of the Civil and Vietnam wars described in stories such as "Midnight and I'm Not Famous Yet" and "Dragged Fighting from the Tomb" is internalized within the knotted psyches of families, friends, and lovers who actualize their resentment and hatred in sarcastic barbs or violent behavior. Donald R. Noble writes that these are "stories of disintegration, disorder, and failure. Many of them are about the collapse of domestic order" (Noble, 42). "Behold the Husband in His Perfect Agony" combines elements of both wartime and domestic battlefields to describe the sudden disintegration of a marriage. Set in Richmond during the Civil War, "Behold the Husband" suggests that warfare between husband and wife is every bit as dangerous and violent as that of a Civil War battlefield. The six-page story is about False Corn, a Huron Indian who is responsible for delivering the message "Jeb Stuart is dead" to Edison, a black contact in Richmond. Throughout the story, as the Yankee

Indian tries to fulfill his mission, he thinks longingly of his wife and child in Baltimore: "On his wrist he wore a light sterling bracelet. It was his wife's and it brought her close to him when he shook it on his arm and felt its tender weight" (*A*, 165). In the lobby of his hotel, he receives a note indicating that he has been betrayed, and that his black contact is dead. Returning to his room, False Corn discovers that his wife Tess is his betrayer and a Confederate, but only after he defeats his adversary with concealed dynamite. His perfect marriage has been an illusion.

Although "Behold the Husband in His Perfect Agony" is set during the Civil War, it actually belongs within the domestic stories in *Airships*. Hannah describes False Corn as the perfect husband, not only because he thinks lovingly of his wife, but also because he has remained faithful to her without a struggle during his travels. Hannah suggests, however, that False Corn's wife, uncertain of her husband's fidelity, resents him more for his possible sexual dalliances than his Northern allegiance. Successfully costumed as a man, she accuses him of keeping other women:

"You have a funny name, a big pistol, and you've been quite a spy. We know all the women you've been with."

"Then you know nothing. I've been with no women."

"Why not? A man gets lonely."

"I've been more hungry than lustful in these parts. I have a wife, a child." (*A*, 162)

But False Corn's wife, who hides her identity and her Confederate alliance from her husband, still attempts to kill him in spite of his honest reaction—a double betrayal. On the landscape of Hannah's domestic battlefield, it is often the girlfriends and wives who consciously destroy their male lovers and husbands. Just as False Corn possesses only partial vision (one of his eyes is destroyed in Atlanta during the war), Hannah's male protagonists in *Airships* are usually sympathetic victims, impaired physically and emotionally by betrayed love.

In "Constant Pain in Tuscaloosa," for example, a deserted husband still receives phone calls from his ex-wife who falsely promises that she may return. She also encourages her present lovers to ridicule her husband's name, Ellsworth, and to describe their sexual exploits to him in detail. Although the wife claims that she is in constant pain, Hannah makes it clear that the husband is the actual victim by emphasizing his reaction to the cruel phone calls: "Actually it tore the last shred out of my bosom. I don't love her, but she was mine, and I don't want anybody else to, either. She knows that,

that's why she called. She wants me to join her in constant pain" (A, 172).
Hannah suggests that his wife's cruelty drives Ellsworth to treat others with
similar disrespect but he actually is looking for new avenues of communication. For example, he insults a black man and his sister, not to drive them
away, but in the hope of inviting them to dinner to alleviate his loneliness.
When they do arrive, he tempts them with steaks, dope, and music, hoping
to encourage them to stay, but when they sit in their Chrysler for temporary,
air-conditioned comfort, Ellsworth worries that they might desert him too:
"I thought it was a ruse to leave for good. When they shut the door, I had to
call back this yell that was coming out of my throat. It was a yell that if it
had come out would've been the weirdest sound I ever made" (A, 174). The
blacks do return, only to "beat the damn light" out of Ellsworth and then
stay to dinner (A, 174). The story ends with Ellsworth expressing love for
the black girl (after knowing her for only one week) while her brother continues to threaten Ellsworth with violence and desertion.

Noble describes the world that Hannah creates in *Airships* as desperate
and pathetic, "a world in which the characters are at the edge. . . . There are
largely funny stories, but it is often gallows humor, as if there is literally
nothing left to do but laugh; conditions are too bleak for anything else"
(Noble, 43). Destroyed by the cruelty of his wife and the constant pain he
experiences, whether caused by his wrecked motorcycle or his wife's phone
calls, Ellsworth is left, as Noble suggests, with nothing but his ability to
laugh at himself and his unhappy situation. But if physical pain is the price
Ellsworth must pay to create an environment free from loneliness and alienation, then he is willing and eager to begin.

Not all of the domestic stories in *Airships* present relationships between
husbands and wives. In "Coming Close to Donna," the most violent of the
domestic tales, Hannah describes the incidental cruelty that occurs within
the midst of casual relationships. Donna, the story's central character, undresses as she excitedly watches her two boyfriends, Hank and Ken, battle
one another in a cemetery to win her affections. Sexually stimulated by the
slugging and pounding, Donna persuades the narrator, Vince, to attempt to
have sex with her: " 'Come in me, you fag,' says she. 'Don't hurt my feelings. I want a fag to come in me' " (A, 46). When the two suitors actually
kill one another over Donna, she absorbs herself "in a tender unnatural act
over the blue jeans of Hank and Ken," but is disappointed at her failed en-
deavor: " 'I can't make anybody come! I'm not good,' she says" (A, 47).
Years later Vince, high on cocaine, meets Donna, gone on heroin, and she
once again pressures him to sleep with her and to take her to the old cemetery. There she undresses, and as she screams to Vince for sexual satisfaction,

he crushes her head with an old tombstone: "Donna wanted what she wanted. I gave it to her" (*A*, 48).

On the domestic battlefield, impotency and dissatisfaction cause violence, and self-hatred manifests itself in destructive behavior toward others. Donna's sense of self-worth is measured by her successful sexual conquests, but her choice of subjects is random and desperate. The title of the story expresses the irony of the narrator's position, and indeed the position of each of Donna's men. Literally, no one comes close to her because she makes no effort to know herself, and, figuratively, no one "comes" within her, which she associates with personal failure. The narrator, Vince, watches her more objectively than most, not only because he may be homosexual, but also because he cares more about not creasing his trousers than he does about making successful sexual advances toward Donna. His violent action at the end of the story *is* kind; he spares Donna from a life of unfulfilled desires and self-destruction. According to Hannah's implied narrative voice in *Airships,* Vince really does give Donna what she wants.

In "Coming Close to Donna" the actual violence in the cemetery parallels that of the battlefield where murder is commonplace and the value placed on life is cheap. But in most of the domestic stories, the violence exhibited is more subtle and calculated. In "Our Secret Home" the Lees throw a party for 65 people and only 12 show, three uninvited. Hannah based this story on an incident that occurred when he was teaching at Clemson University: "There was a person who threw a party and nobody came. That's an old joke, but I was one of the three guests who showed up. It was terribly embarrassing. The hors d'oeuvres had been set out, the liquor was expensive and plentiful, and everything was primed for his friends to show, but they didn't. I was edgy for him and embarrassed" (Gretland, 232). In the story, although most guests "invited were lushes who normally wouldn't pass up cocktails at the home of Hitler," they avoid the Lees, more because of the husband and narrator Mickey than his wife Carolyn (*A*, 119). Mickey learns he is at fault from a guest, Mrs. Craft, who obviously has no idea that he is the host. She speaks openly about a couple whom everyone deserted for laying the fault on the husband in that situation too: "He suddenly changed. He went bad. A handsome devil too. But we couldn't stand him after the change" (*A*, 122).

In the Lees' case, Mickey's feebleminded sister Patricia is the reason their friends are quitting them. She lives upstairs and frightens guests during social functions as she roams around the house. As one couple states after spending a few minutes kissing in the study: "Even sex wouldn't be any good *here*" (*A*, 123). When the 12 guests filter out and Carolyn deserts

Mickey for a resentful, drunken sleep, he escapes into Patricia's room where he bathes her and shaves her armpits. The attraction between them is obvious, and Hannah hints strongly at possibilities of incest. In bed later, Carolyn refuses to hear what occurred upstairs with her husband and sister-in-law: "Don't tell me what went on. I don't want to know. I love you too much to do anything about it" (A, 127). When Carolyn refuses to sleep with him, he seeks solace in old love letters his sister wrote him after he taught her speech and writing skills: "My essence yearned and rose from the closet and my roots tore from me, standing up like a tangled tree in dark heaven" (A, 128). In the midst of this sexual fantasy, Mickey dreams of leaving Washington, D. C., and academia for the South, new friends, privacy, maybe even the Democratic party. Hannah ends the story with Mickey discovering a selfish answer to his problems: he daydreams of a life by the sea with his wife and his sister living in peaceful harmony, a solution that would alienate them from further contact with the outside world and inevitably separate husband and wife.

The cruelty exhibited by the Lees' guests Hannah explains by the dishonest relationship between friends and lovers. Rather than express the truth that Patricia makes them uncomfortable, the Lees' guests resort to whispered threats and idle rumors. Like Donna in "Coming Close to Donna," Mickey Lee is a character no one comes close to. Carolyn, his wife, is blinded by love and Patricia, his sister, is too mentally disturbed to offer any advice. Abandoned by friends and family, Mickey fantasizes about changes that will not occur. Unlike Donna, Mickey has no friend like Vince to end his dilemma with a cemetery tombstone; instead, he is doomed to an isolated existence as social outcast, inspiring people to stop talking and stare whenever he enters a room. Carolyn Lee is not the perpetrator of revenge or desertion, like the wives in "Behold the Husband in His Perfect Agony" and "Constant Pain in Tuscaloosa"; rather, Carolyn sins through weakness. She loves her husband unconditionally and is too weak to encourage change or to offer options. She chooses to ignore the situation, punishing her husband by refusing sexual favors, ironically pushing him closer to his disturbed sister.

In "Love Too Long" the narrator's obsessive love for his ex-wife Jane exceeds Mickey's for his sister in "Our Secret Home." Without Jane, he loses the ability to hold a job, to keep a friend, to do anything more than remain in his deserted house and move from chair to chair, nervously waiting for his wife to pilot her airplane over his neighborhood. Hannah describes the husband in "Love Too Long" as one of the most scatterbrained and self-deceptive of all of the characters in *Airships,* unable to remember the author of *The Canterbury Tales* or to figure out that his wife is unfaithful to him with movie producers, architects, and librarians. He blindly and humorously dismisses her infidelities, claiming, "She was never unfaithful to me that I know. And if I knew it, I wouldn't care because I know she's sworn to me" (*A*, 10). But the story itself contradicts the narrator's aloofness. The narrator jealously recounts his wife's houseboat trip with a movie star making a comeback in South Carolina, her dinner with an architect designing for her a free dream house, and her LSD trip with professors and librarians working at the University of Florida. Although the narrator and Jane have twice married and divorced, their life together as husband and wife was uneventful, even by the husband's account: a series of false pregnancies, rainy days, and severe headaches.

Eventually the narrator resents Christianity for not curing his obsessive, destructive love for Jane. First, he wishes he *was* Jesus, "somebody who never drank or wanted nooky. Or knew Jane" (*A*, 12). Then he challenges God with threats he makes about the hyprocrisy of his behavior: " 'You great bastard!' I yelled up there. 'I believed in You on and off all my life. There better be something up there like Jane or I'll humiliate you! I'll swine myself all over this town. I'll appear in public places and embarrass the shit out of You, screaming that I'm a Christian!' " (*A*, 15). Ultimately, the narrator in "Love Too Long" fails at each of his endeavors because, he, like other characters in *Airships,* leads a life without order, balance, or identity. He allows Jane to become everything to him: "Nothing in the world matters but you and your woman. Friendship and politics go to hell" (*A*, 15). But Hannah maintains humor in the story, as Allen Shepherd suggests, "by a combination of sheer manic inventiveness and formulaic sequences in which bad plus worse somehow always equals worst. Predictability conditions empathy" (Shepherd, 67). The humor originates not only from the narrator's comic inability to recognize truth, but primarily from his manic, unsuccessful efforts at reconciliation. The reader soon realizes that Jane, not the ex-husband, is the real victim in "Love Too Long," one who fortunately escapes the clutches of a man who bases his sense of self-worth and identity on her existence. At the end of the story the narrator wonders why his wife flies her plane over their house: "Is she saying she wants me so much she'd pay for a plane to my yard? Or is she saying: Look at this, I never gave a damn for anything but fun in the air?" (*A*, 15). The answer is obviously neither. Jane flies to express her well-deserved independence from a parasite who seeks to suck her identity from her in order to feed one of his own.

On the domestic battleground, Hannah does allow for love between couples, but even they are not exempt from causal and accidental destructiveness within the family. In "Deaf and Dumb" Minny, Daryl, and their four children suffer financially because of Daryl's overt honesty in the real estate business. Although Minny demonstrated promise as an art student in college, she has sacrificed her future for her family and her husband—but she is not filled with regret: "But I loved Daryl and his pride. I guess I have pride. I guess I'm lucky how much I love Daryl, who's a silly ass by any judgment. . . . Daryl is my hobby" (A, 180). She appreciates the honesty between them, and their good sexual intercourse she views as a work of art. Occasionally overcome by the responsibility of managing a large family on a small budget, Minny is one of the more satisfied characters in Airships; her life is not what she would want it to be, but she seems moderately happy. When she returns exhausted from grocery shopping, she falls asleep with her youngest child by her side, remembering past suitors and dreaming of Daryl.

The violence that interrupts the lives of Minny and Daryl in "Deaf and Dumb" occurs through no real fault of their own. Daryl, returning home from having had only one beer after work, opens the wrong door and tumbles down the rotten basement stairs, while the boys bring into the mother's room a king snake they have knocked unconscious with a hammer. The youngest boy, believing that it is a sin for his mother to sleep in the afternoon, hits her in the mouth with a hammer, jarring the king snake awake: "It rose and twisted since half its nerves were gone. It almost stood up" (A, 181). The story ends with the mother, who upon seeing the snake, believes herself to be dreaming, and feels guilt because of her slumber. Like the deaf and dumb mute selling pens whom Minny once ridiculed in New Orleans, the couples' lives seem directionless and uncontrollable. Families create responsibility; responsibility, guilt; and guilt, pressure.

In the domestic stories in Airships Hannah suggests that relationships, even those based on mutual love as in "Deaf and Dumb," lose their uphill battle to overcome the tendency toward disorder and violent disintegration. In his review of Airships in the New York Times Book Review, Michael Wood pointed to the inevitable comparison between the situation in "Deaf and Dumb" and that in Eden: "It would be crude to look for allegory here, and I'm not sure we need even to labor for meaning at all, once we have fixed the elements of this vision in our minds. Dream, drink, husband, wife, snake, heat, home say all we need to know" (Wood, 35). In spite of their efforts and apparent affection for one another, Daryl and Minny will remain unsatisfied. On a literal level, they must predict and overcome the incidental violence that threatens their existence; on a figurative level, they must combat the failures of Adam and Eve in the Garden of Eden.

The Internal Battlefield

The third type of warfare explored in *Airships* is fought within the minds of characters. Although Hannah uses a first-person narrator in almost all of the stories, the more surreal tales in the collection present a less recognizable reality and are usually restricted to either the confines of the narrator's memory or the juxtaposed, contradictory views of several perspectives. In "Quo Vadis, Smut?" for example, Hannah creates a dense narrative that parallels a roped bull with a lout named Reggy John (whose sweetheart Betsy appears mysteriously tied naked to the underside of the animal). In the story, the narrator, Colonel Feather, several privates, and Sergeant Leet kill and skin the bull, keep Reggy John and his prostitute captive, and take over Farmer Lutz's barn for shelter. The time and the place are unspecified and unimportant. The soldier, the captured couple, and the farmer vaguely discuss murdered women and the insignificance of death, but the narrative never progresses conventionally toward a resolution. Leet argues with captured prisoner Reggy John on their flight to Atlanta that death is *something:* "Generally it means the end of what good you can do your fellow man," to which John replies, "There ain't no fellow man but me" (*A,* 64). To exact revenge, Leet introduces John to a drink that will eventually lead him to a fate worse than death—insatiable and uncontrollable addiction:

The taste is exquisite but there are flakes of glass in the gin. They burn constantly but do not kill. Elimination can become a problem. John, who was thirsty, would last many years with it. The drink creates a slavish thirst for the next drink. It calms the need for six hours. Then the great thirst comes again. He drank it. The man thinks he is an alcoholic but the need is much worse than that.

He will come crawling back to us forever and we will give him the drink and kick him out. (A, 64)

Even the forms of torture in "Quo Vadis, Smut?" are unrealistic and contrived; the success of Leet's "martini" depends on John's unlikely ability to locate the soldier forever, but Hannah implies that this is possible, and indeed, probable.

Other elements in the story seem purposely improbable and vague: Colonel Wooten leaves with Reggy John's sweetheart Betsy, touched by her tale of woe; Atlanta is a city without policemen or a security force; Reggy John writes poetry equating beauty with death; and Farmer Lutz is excited about introducing his wife and children to the intruding soldiers. The last three paragraphs especially illustrate Hannah's tendency in the internal tales in

Airships to juxtapose segments unrelated temporally, spatially, and contextually to imitate the associational nature of memory. Only Colonel Feather's
narrative voice makes the story a coherent whole. As he returns home (at
some unspecified, futuristic time and place), now rich and important, he
finds his wife drenched in perfume and within a veil waiting for him in front
of a burning fire: "On her feet are silver sandals. Her rear is raised. She has
her face on a cushion of velvet . . . knees on the rug, rear high, and
overcomingly sweet with perfume. She says darling darling darling" (*A*,
65). With no mention of the soldiers, Reggy John, or the war, Colonel
Feather ends the story by confessing, "This is my fifth wife. Lucky for me at
last I got the right one" (*A*, 65).

Although the narrative is confusing and purposely misleading, the driving force behind "Quo Vadis, Smut?" is clear: immediate gratification is the
ultimate goal of almost every character in this futuristic tale. Farmer Lutz's
wife greedily grabs money from the soldiers for the family's trouble; the
Corporal abducts the prostitute for his own pleasure; Reggy John laps
thirstily at Colonel Wooten's addictive drink; the soldiers kill and hungrily
devour a bull; and Colonel Feather takes his wife anally to prove his financial success. Juxtaposing the domestic ending of "Quo Vadis, Smut?" to the
war account gives the story a sense of timelessness, and illustrates that war
simply brings out in its participants cannibalistic qualities that exist always
beneath the surface of civilization. The acquisitive, insensitive nature of
Feather, his desire for ownership and possession, is illustrated both by his
need for verbal appreciation from his men and total submission from his
wife. The irony, of course, is that even though he scoffs at Corporal
Wooten's desire for John's whorish girlfriend, Colonel Feather possesses little more than a veiled, harem slave at the end of "Quo Vadis, Smut?" He
may set himself above the primitive responses of those around him, but
Feather is no more civilized or advanced. At the end of the story, Feather ac-
quires what is important to him: money, power, and consistent, unthinking
sexual gratification.

Although "Green Gets It" is more focused on one central perspective
than "Quo Vadis, Smut?," it still presents a similar almost surreal internal
landscape of the mind. "Green Gets It" describes the last few days in the life
of Quarles Green ("his parents wanted to compensate for the last name with
a fancy first one"), a 70-year-old government worker who dies at the end of
the story in a plane en route to Memphis to visit one of the few friends who
may remember him. The story traces several events in Green's life, related
only by violence and perseverance: his fall off of a party yacht into the
Hudson River; his unsatisfactory carnal experiences; his unhappy marriage

to a woman who left him to join Billy Graham's World Crusade; and his wormlike existence after leaving the South for ten years. But it is the nonsensical nature of the violence and not the randomness of events he encounters that really seems unnatural.

The first "victim" of Green's violent nature was supposedly a "stiller" (a person who operates an illegal distillery) locked in a hooch shack, Weeber Batson's oldest son. The second was a 70-year-old Indian who purportedly served under Geronimo and shot Green in the solar plexis with an arrow. The third was a negro who recognized Green's federal affiliation and broke the miscegenation law. Hannah's efforts to imitate stylistically Green's associationist thought processes justify the story's tendency to juxtapose without detailed explanation one incident to another. For example, Green jumps from the death of Batson's son to his wife's tendency to mother him during sickness, to the Indian reservation:

The guys kept calling him just a stiller, but I knew better and I was sick at heart. Oh, she really got interested in me when I was sick. That's when she comes alive, going around with cold towels and that cold mud porridge. . . . When I got well, we were in Arizona holding down the corn beer production on the Apache reservation. It suited me. I didn't want to be near Mobile again. And on the reservation there was a drunk Indian I shot. (A, 100)

Although at 70 Green says he is fit and healthy, Hannah illustrates the decaying, untrustworthy nature of the protagonist's memory by presenting associational memories that make sense only to the narrator himself. Within the scope of Quarles Green's mind, the word "sick" leads him from memories of the stiller to those of his wife's obsessive care, and the Apache reservation near their home in Arizona reminds him more of a murdered Indian than of his life out West. "Green Gets It" is essentially a journey of the mind, leaving the reader wondering which elements are reliable and which are products of a senile, overactive imagination.

In the final page of the story Hannah shifts from first to third person to describe the death of Green and to put the story in a sharper perspective. As Quarles sits in the plane headed toward Memphis eyeing the stewardess and experiencing his last pangs of sexual desire, "a terrific fist bash[es] him directly on the heart" (A, 104). His death is as casual as his memory: "He sat there awhile and died . . . a tight smug smile on him, his eyes closed, like every dead man who finally hears his tune" (A, 104). Green does "get" what he wants. His life has been a random, purposeless string of unhappy memories. Only at his death when Green feels peace or at least an absence of pain does Hannah allow the reader to achieve an honest, evaluative distance from the character's mind. Green's death is ironically the only event recounted in the story that is entirely believable.

In the final story in *Airships,* "Mother Rooney Unscrolls the Hurt," Hannah borrows characters and incidents from *Geronimo Rex* to describe once again the intimacy and unreliability of memory. Ancient Mother Rooney, landlady to Harry Monroe, Bobby Dove Fleece, and Jerry Silas of *Geronimo Rex,* tumbles down the stairs of her boardinghouse, only to be stopped from plunging through the kitchen door to her death by a brooch she wears. Acting as a brake, the brooch prevents her from moving past the staircase, but, in the process, sinks firmly three inches into her bosom, providing the opportunity for Mother Rooney, like Quarles Green, to explore the past: "She lay hurt more than she knew beside the stairs, and felt only as usual, surrounded by the towering vacant wings of her house. Now this horror that she had not personally cultivated at all, this queer renewal of sights and sounds in the air—ghosts—was with her" (*A,* 187). She jumps from memories of her rude, destructive boarders to those of her husband Hoover, dead since 1947, and those of the Royal Theatre and Millsaps College. In fact, she keeps herself alive by consciously recounting incidents from her past in her own mind: "she might make her brain like a scroll, and that by just the tiniest bit of mental activity she might pull it down in tiny snatches at a time and dwell on the inch that was offered by the smallest tug of the will, like the scrolled maps in schoolrooms" (*A,* 192). She reviews everything from her painful loss of virginity and her conversion to Irish Catholicism to her son's airplane crash and her eventual isolation.

Mother Rooney's peculiar situation provides a chronological, intimate look at a life full of hardships, one in which constant pain at least reminds her that she is, indeed, alive. Her need for companionship and affection drives her into a violent marriage and an unrewarding profession, but even facing death she possesses pride and self-respect. Unlike Green, Mother Rooney has experienced love and need, and although Hannah makes it clear that others, from her husband to her son to each of her boarders, have victimized her, she has escaped unscathed. At the end of the story, when Mother Rooney is rescued by Harriman Monroe, she walks proudly by herself to the ambulance. When Silas, an old boarder, appears carrying an old drunk on his back and fighting with Monroe, he injures both of them enough to add two more patients to the hospital's ambulance service: "One of the ambulance men had to go in and break off Silas from Monroe, and now Monroe was another case, and Mother Rooney sat beside him and petted him, all the way to the hospital" (*A,* 209). Hannah ends *Airships* optimistically. The

violence inspired by Mother Rooney's fall and Silas's entrance ironically fulfills Mother Rooney's maternal need to care for and protect those around
her. Although he was her least considerate and most critical boarder,
Harriman Monroe becomes husband and son to Mother Rooney as they
ride together to the hospital.

Like "Quo Vadis, Smut?" and "Green Gets It," "Mother Rooney Unscrolls the Hurt" has an unreliable narrator describing questionable incidents. Unlike the stories of actual warfare or those within a domestic
setting, the internal stories present conflicts that are more subtle than
those that exist among couples, families, and friends; instead, those tales
in *Airships* that remain in the protagonists' minds explore the relationships between the past and the present and between fulfilled and unfulfilled expectations. In "Quo Vadis, Smut?" Colonel Feather must search
the past to justify the extent of his materialistic success; in "Green Gets It"
Quarles Green must review his life to look for a reason to continue; and in
"Mother Rooney Unscrolls the Hurt" the landlady must unscroll her history to dismiss it and begin again. By juxtaposing the memories of these
characters, Hannah describes the process of thought and the possibility of
redemption.

Only Mother Rooney in *Airships,* the final character in the collection,
manages to overcome her dismal life to find a hope reminiscent of Thorpe
Trove's in *Nightwatchmen* and Harriman Monroe's in *Geronimo Rex.* She is
literally born again from her near-fatal accident, able to overcome the land-
bound obstacles that have created her exile to reach toward someone she sees
in pain. In many ways, Mother Rooney is the only true "airship" in the collection. She may have lived her life much like the other characters in the
collection—following an almost chartered route with the conviction to
break free—but her brush with death breaks the pattern, figuratively free-
ing Mother Rooney from herself. She is airborne, not only to explore memories of the past, but, more importantly, to change the direction of the
present and the future. She has risen above herself and reexamined her lot,
overcoming obstructions initially created by circumstance. Although her triumph may only be temporary, Mother Rooney has indeed unscrolled her
hurt, and Hannah gives her the courage and honesty to overcome the
wounds inflicted by life.

Chapter Three

The Fragmentation of Experience: *Ray* and *The Tennis Handsome*

In his interview with R. Vanarsdall, Barry Hannah stated, "I just don't care about plot that much, so I have got to have a voice or tone that is going to carry the thing. . . . The kind of tone I want is sometimes just a confluence of music" (Vanarsdall, 326). In his fourth and fifth full-length works, *Ray* (1980) and *The Tennis Handsome* (1983), Hannah abandons the reliance on plot illustrated in *Geronimo Rex* and *Nightwatchmen* for the techniques of fragmentation and disjunctiveness exhibited in the "internal" stories of *Airships*. Each novel illustrates a new direction for Hannah's fiction. Seldom in works following *Ray* will plot play a significant role in Hannah's novels and short stories; instead, he begins to break conventional spatial and temporal novelistic restrictions to create a style imitating the internal thoughts and conflicts of his narrators.

Ray: The Contradictions of a Healer

Eliot Fremont-Smith, in his review "Hoo-Ray," wrote that *Ray* is primarily "the recollection and musings—sorrows and ecstasies, dreams and encounters of a bright, horny 33-year-old Alabama doctor . . . who sings and hums (occasionally yells) us through the book in both first and third persons."[1] Hannah admits that he forwent "physical geography" in *Ray* to concentrate on speech and action resembling tunnel vision, and that after he finished the book he recovered from alcoholism in a California hospital: "The *Ray* thing was pretty true as far as emotions go and after the book came out, at that point in my life, I had just about lost confidence" (Vanarsdall, 326–27). Hannah wrote *Ray* during one of the hottest summers he can remember, directly after a difficult separation and divorce: "Deep angst, trying to cope, and everything in writing was true emotionally. The events didn't all happen, but in the psyche they did" (Vanarsdall, 327).

The experimental structure of *Ray,* then, attempts not only to delineate the thought processes of a doctor facing a crisis of the self, but also to describe Hannah's own inability to make sense of reality during one of the more emotionally stressful periods of his life.

In *Ray* Hannah describes the life of Ray Forrest, who like the narrator in "Water Liars," is facing his thirty-third year, the age at which Christ was crucified. In a Mobile, Alabama, hospital, "drying out" from alcohol abuse and drug addiction, Ray uses his mind to "think himself" free from his claustrophobic situation.[2] Although *Ray* chronologically traces the narrator from his stay in Mobile through a series of seriocomic tragedies to a position of strength and affirmation, its reliance on both first- and third-person narration and its 62 juxtaposed prose segments imitate the confusing internal musings of a man randomly reviewing his life to learn to accept himself and the world around him. In his review of *Ray* Harry Crews defined this prose juxtaposition as Ray's "tendency to float. He drifts into other people's minds and lives, into the deep past, the Civil War for instance."[3] Hannah forces his readers to become prisoners of Ray's active imagination and rampant bigotry. Fighting to maintain or determine chronological sequence is useless and counterproductive: Ray's life is distinguished not by the progression of his thoughts but by the value and integrity of his observations and memories.

To trace the associational process of Ray's memory and to stress his dual roles as narrator and subject, Hannah uses both first- and third-person narration. This technique gives Ray the freedom to recount his own interpretation of specific choices that make up his life, but it also allows enough distance for Hannah to clarify the irony in Ray's decisions and machinations; in other words, in first person Ray admonishes the reader and chastises himself, while in third person he attempts to separate himself from his life in order to analyze it objectively. This technique offers an in-depth study of the psyche of one man, and, as Crews suggests, it "very nearly merges reader and experience, greatly diminishing the distance that has always separated the two" (Crews, 4). Time and space in the novel depend on what Ray wants the reader to remember. The novel begins with Ray in a period of self-query, reminding himself of his situation while describing his predicament: "Ray you are a doctor and you are in a hospital in Mobile, except now you are a patient but you're still me. Say what? You say you want to know who I am?" (*Ray,* 3). His subsequent tale explains and justifies his dilemma both to satisfy his acknowledged audience and to assuage his own guilt.

The driving force behind reading the novel is not the search for answers to the question "What happens next?"; instead, as Walter Clemons pointed out, "*Ray* is a novel of brilliant particulars, dizzying juxtaposition, and no reassuring narrative transition."[4] Benjamin DeMott, in his review of *Ray* for the *New York Times Book Review,* admitted that "plot-wise *Ray* is not one of your page turners,"[5] and Michael Malone of the *Nation* believed that Hannah subordinates Ray's life to concentrate on "voices" that make *Ray* "a speedboat on the big lake of Southern fiction":[6] "Voices: lyric, lewd, sly, spooked, tawdry, an oratory of hyperbolic Southern voices; voices and not plots or themes are what the Muses whisper to him. . . . Ray's life gets lived, but we hear it in the background: his voice is louder and larger" (Malone, 585). Donald R. Noble, who believes that *Ray* is Hannah's most successful critical and commercial work, writes that "not only is there no conventional narrative flow, there is no regard for *time,* much less chronology" (Noble, 43). Although he employs similar techniques in short stories from *Airships,* such as "Mother Rooney Unscrolls the Hurt" and "Green Gets It," *Ray* marks Hannah's first successful effort at juxtaposing unrelated segments of one man's life with little attention paid to temporal and spatial continuity.

Most critics reacted enthusiastically to Hannah's experimental work of fiction. DeMott called *Ray* "the funniest, weirdest, soul-happiest work of fiction by a genuinely young American author that I've read in a long while," and Harry Crews wrote that *Ray* "has the kind of unity and coherence that we associate with the best fiction" (DeMott, 4). Michael Malone compared the novel to Eudora Welty's *The Ponder Heart* and Flannery O'Connor's *The Violent Bear It Away,* and Geoffrey Wolff said that the novel has "energy, acuity of observation, stamina, formal beauty, wit."[7] But Benjamin De Mott paid *Ray* the greatest compliment by pointing not only to its similarities to works by O'Connor, Byrne, Barthelme, and Pynchon, but, more significantly, to its differences: "Barry Hannah's cruelty is better-natured than Hunter Thompson's; his people are less abstract than Donald Barthelme's . . . his repugnance at shopping mall U.S.A. is more energizing than David Byrne's . . . his playful linkages of aeronautical and sexual behavior are more exhilarating than Pynchon's" (DeMott, 7). As so many critics suggest, the success of *Ray* lies in its truthful portrayal of a doctor who is an adulterer, a murderer, and a conceited prig, and in Hannah's ability to create a novelistic form that perfectly reflects the complex psyche of the major character.

Hannah begins *Ray* with a 23-page section that provides selected background information about the major character, while simultaneously introducing the experimental structure of the novel. In this first segment Hannah illustrates Ray's tendency to jump from memory to memory without preparing for the break in continuity. After humorously admonishing himself for the problems that landed him in the alcohol and drug abuse clinic, Ray describes his relationship with the Hooches, a large family living in abject poverty among broken cans, rotting brassieres, misshapen drain-pipes, and soaked food. His interest in the Hooches is focused upon his ad-miration for Mr. Hooch, the poetry-writing father, Mrs. Hooch, the morphine-addicted mother, and especially Sister, their promiscuous and attractive daughter with whom Ray builds a relationship based on sex, drugs, and mutual respect. Ray describes their first meeting and initial sex-ual relationships, and then jumps abruptly to the story of Charlie De Soto, manager of a soap factory in Tuscaloosa, Charlie's relationship with his sweetheart Eileen, and his comic disagreement with his irritatingly precise neighbor Mr. Wently. Ray makes no real attempt to tie the tales together. At the end of the first section he says simply that "this was all when I was thirty-three and divorced" (*Ray*, 26), a statement that neither defends the narrative attention paid to the Hooches and De Soto and nor attempts to explain their significance in his life.

In the next few segments of the novel Hannah illustrates that it is primar-ily through Ray's "good ole' boy" ramblings, both in first and third person, that readers begin to understand him. Hannah combines factual informa-tion about Ray's life—his background as an ex–navy pilot in Vietnam, his second marriage to the feisty and independent Westy, his background in fine arts—with the prejudices and emotional reactions that drive his life: his distrust of doctors and their children, his fear of venereal disease, his weak-ness for sexual liaisons, and his dread of dependencies of any kind. Ray jumps as rapidly from third to first person as he does from past to present incidents in his life: "Ray even teaches a popular night class at the university now. It's open to just about anybody except people I don't like or think I won't" (*Ray*, 27). And within these jumbled segments of self-confession and story telling, Hannah juxtaposes a series of one- to five-line sections, resem-bling Faulkner's brief and enigmatic chapters in *As I Lay Dying*. These short segments flesh out Hannah's complex portrayal of the psyche of one man by interrupting the narrative to introduce some philosophical point or psychological belief. In these brief segments, which resemble cinematic montage, Hannah flashes for the reader brief images, both concrete and ab-stract, that Ray finds significant. Segment 5, for example, justifies Ray's leaps in temporal and spatial continuity: "I live so many centuries. Every-body is still alive" (*Ray*, 41). It prepares the reader for Ray's belief in rein-carnation and prefigures Ray's tendency to place himself within several centuries simultaneously. In segment 11 Ray comically emphasizes his pride in his sexuality: "Whoever created Ray gave him a big sex engine. I live near the Black Warrior River and have respect for things" (*Ray*, 46). And in segment 52 he summarizes the three most important facets of Ray's life, which serve as the contextual basis for the novel: "To live and delight in healing, flying, fucking" (*Ray*, 98).

Whatever digressions Ray may make within his tale, he usually returns to narrative lines expressing one of these three facets, less to define himself than to emphasize his ultimate isolation; ironically, the more readers learn about Ray, the less they like or respect him. Ray *is* a healer, for example, but identifies with none of the other doctors with whom he comes into contact. In segment 2 Ray lists the people he likes—those who work on foreign cars, botanists, geologists, wrestlers, and tennis players—and those he dislikes: "But a category of worst is doctors' children in revolt. Give me an honest nigger any time of day. I'll even read his essays" (*Ray*, 27). When speaking of his second wife's brother, an orthopedic surgeon in Omaha, he admits, "There is no escape from doctors. They surround me as I surround myself" (*Ray*, 31). Although Ray's lack of pretense about the medical profession is admirable, he embodies an entirely different set of conceits. He uses his status as healer to set himself above and beyond conventional morality even though he is often in the position of healing those whom he has hurt himself. He not only exchanges addictive drugs such as morphine with the Hooches for sexual favors from their daughter, but his research concentrates primarily on medical problems that ironically exploit the suffering of his female patients or directly serve himself: "The Nervous Woman and Valium," "Three Seraxes a Day for the Alcoholic," "Satyriasis and Acute Depression" (*Ray*, 26). He even uses his position as healer to encourage his nurse Rebecca to act as a sexual instrument for healing his friend Charlie De Soto's acute gastritis over a peptic ulcer: "Rebecca puts the needle in him. . . . She looks at me quickly. She takes down the top of her uniform. The large dark-nippled breasts are there. Charlie is lying in the leather chair and she lowers herself to him. . . . In three weeks his ulcer was cured. . . . He told me he paid Rebecca for a week but all the rest was free" (*Ray*, 69). Hannah describes Ray as a healer, but his unorthodox methods and his disregard for professional ethics and personal morality isolate him from the medical community and from his acknowledged audience.

Probably most indicative of Ray's God complex as a healer is an incident in which he chooses to kill a patient he could easily save. Adopting third-person narration in a subtle effort to separate himself from the deed, Ray recounts, "But Ray confesses he deliberately lost the bastard who was eighty" (*Ray*, 70). A wife- and a child-beater, the 80-year-old patient is in intensive care suffering from a heart attack. When Ray discovers that the old man plans to attack his family when recovered, he engineers the man's death: "I yanked out the connections and shut down the monitor and let him pass over the light into hell. By the time the crew came in, I had all kind of stuff going again" (*Ray,* 71). This "murder" introduces a contradiction of morality that extends throughout the novel: Ray's patient may indeed deserve to die, but Ray alone does not have the right to assess the degree of punishment the wife-beater should receive. Symbolically, Ray is killing the side of himself that unreasonably and violently lashes out at those people with whom he disagrees, but contextually, Ray exhibits his tendency to confuse his responsibilities as healer with those of judge. Ray believes in his own abilities not only to heal others, but also to determine their right to be healed.

Flying, the second facet of Ray's existence that he admittedly lives for, illustrates that, like other Hannah protagonists, Ray associates violence with pleasure. An ex-navy pilot who flew support missions for B-52 bombers in Vietnam, Ray consistently juxtaposes segments of his life as a fighter with those of his civilian life as a healer. He describes himself in macho-heroic terms. Whether he is saving a DC-8 headed to Birmingham from crashing while placing an order for a second martini, or turning the nose of his aircraft, the Phantom, almost perpendicular to the ground to rescue his Mississippi friend Quisenberry from a horde of "gooks," Ray is always bolstering his image to both his audience and himself by recounting his successes in combat. And he does not limit these successes to his stint in the navy; he carries over the same principles of violent survival into his daily routine. He imagines himself as the lone defender of an almost cinematic heroic ideal, a fighter who acts for justice first and asks questions later. Hannah manipulates the readers by making Ray's victims moral degenerates, people supposedly deserving their violent fate:

But I still want to fight. I still want to put it to somebody, duke a big guy out. Like the asshole who came in who had shot two of his children and broken the arm of his wife. He was an alcoholic red-neck and had a lot of Beechnut chewing tobacco on him. He smelled really lousy. Before I could ask him anything, he found a razor blade and came at *me,* his doctor! Lucky that Ray still had his quickness. The bastard missed me with the razor, and I kicked him in the gonads. (*Ray,* 43)

Ray is careful always to set himself up in these violent scenes as the sole crusader to right wrongs—he defeats those whom he feels deserve the beating. But the reader realizes that those whom Ray physically destroys are no more

48   BARRY HANNAH

degenerate than the doctor himself. Ray may contend that "one lesson we as
Americans must learn is to get used to the contrarieties in our hearts and
learn to live with them," but he exhibits neither the patience nor the intelligence to live by such a philosophy (*Ray*, 51). Rather, his actions reflect the
impetuousness and violence of his immediate needs, not the intelligence of
his thoughts.

In his civilian life Ray ironically resorts to violence as a method of preserving Southern gentility and good taste. When a former student from his
American civilization class approaches him with a poem after Sister's murder trial, for example, Ray uncontrollably slugs him, more to protect the
Southern literary image than to right any apparent wrong: "They always say
Southerners can write. So I slugged this skinny lad. I laid him down the
steps. . . . I duked away this harmless poet" (*Ray*, 55). The student's primary crime is not tactlessness, but lack of poetic ability. Ray resorts to a
similar solution when he discovers that a Sigma Chi brother is responsible
for attacking his friend Charlie de Soto's drunken uncle in the park: "I
bashed the fuck out of his ribs . . . and his grandmother screamed. We put
them both in the ambulance. I healed everybody" (*Ray*, 65). Ray is careful
to admit only to violence that he describes as justifiable, and he emphasizes
the fact that medical training at Tulane allows him to heal the wrongs he
commits. But his many acts of violence distance him from readers, causing
them to judge him as harshly as he judges others.

As in *Airships*, the gallantry of the Old South as embodied by Jeb Stuart
also drives Ray to commit violent acts, all in the service of humanity, justice,
and the Southern way of life. Benjamin DeMott writes of the effectiveness
of the Civil War sections in *Ray*: "The odd Civil War fragments interspersed
throughout *Airships*, Hannah's extraordinary collection of short stories, are
shrewdly worked into the texture of this new book, setting up resonances
with the Vietnam experience that weren't fully felt in *Airships*" (DeMott,
7). Certainly, the Civil War experience described in *Ray*, tracing the gallant
efforts of soldiers fruitlessly fighting for a dying civilization, clearly parallels
the Vietnam incidents chronicling Ray's adventures as an ex–navy pilot.
The Jeb Stuart tales detailing the final efforts of the Confederacy implicitly
criticize the less gallant behavior of soldiers during the Vietnam War by emphasizing the loss of honor and respect exhibited by a nation that neither
believed in nor understood its cause. The Vietnam segments of *Ray* are almost always more graphically violent than the Civil War sections, and
Hannah heightens the fear and prejudice apparent in the latter war that was
missing in the Confederate cause. For example, Ray's description of his
Vietnam experience reflects its lack of order and devaluation of life: "I've

got the .32 machine pistol that I killed a gook in the head with. . . . We were all fueling at Ton Sa Nut. Fifteen F-4's all in line. You couldn't ever kill enough of them. Vietnam was like fleas" (*Ray*, 73). Section 29 even recounts a war code indecipherable to the reader without military experience: "ERD. #92. #Doc 4. Utap. At 40–50. Range. In Clear. Solid. Ventro" (*Ray*, 80). In contrast, section 50, describing an incident in the Civil War, stresses the soldier's confusion, but, unlike the Vietnam segments, emphasizes the soldier's sacrifice and bravery:

Your hat's rotting off. It's hot. You're not sure about your horse or the cause. All you know is that you are here—through the clover, through the low-hanging branch, through the grapeshot.
  All of it missed you.
Your saber is up, and there goes your head, Christian. (*Ray*, 96)

Hannah uses the Civil War stories to heighten the heroic tendencies of the lone Southern soldier fighting to protect more than just his concrete love of country; rather, the Confederate soldiers were attempting to preserve an abstract ideal: the honor and nobility of an agrarian way of life.

Ray, who claims early in the novel that his life has spanned centuries, sets himself up as a physical embodiment of the contradictory tendencies of both wars. Only Ray, who is reincarnated from the earlier war, understands the necessity of preserving the gentility of the Civil War within the Vietnam War skirmishes. His transition from the present to the past is purposely abrupt, and he places himself directly within the Civil War not as an observer but as a participant: "Jeb Stuart is as weary as the rest of us, but he calls for sabers out. Our uniforms are rotting off us. He's so hot and this gray cloth is so hot" (*Ray*, 39). In section 20 Ray recounts his own death and the demise of his fellow soldiers, a model of foolish bravery and Southern gentility, and then he didactically emphasizes its significance when compared to the less illustrious wars of today:

There is no turning back. Hold sabers. We will walk to them until they shoot and then we will charge.
  Everybody was killed. One Union private lived to tell the story.
  If warriors had known this story, we would have taken the war to the gooks with more dignity. (*Ray*, 66)

For Ray, flying and fighting are synonymous. Healing provides no thrill equal to the excitement of physical combat, in spite of its ability to raise Ray to the level of hero, unless it too involves the violence, sacrifice, honor, and dignity exhibited by soldiers from the Civil War. In *Airships,* Hannah uses Stuart paradoxically to symbolize foolish dignity; in *Ray,* Hannah emphasizes the nobility of Stuart's career and the strength of his convictions. Ray excuses Stuart's failure as a general by suggesting that the honor of Stuart's intentions overshadows the foolishness of his actions, which is also the reasoning he employs to rationalize his own mistakes as a husband, healer, and soldier. Aligning the Civil and Vietnam wars, and placing himself in the middle of both, gives Ray a method to justify his love of flying and fighting. He can exhibit his southern/macho tendency to boast of his physical prowess, while binding this love of violence to a sense of gentility and moral righteousness.

The third and possibly most significant facet of Ray's life that gives him reason to live and to delight—"fucking"—represents the weakness that paradoxically enriches and destroys the quality of Ray's life. Sister, daughter of the morphine-addicted Hooches, is the woman Ray loves most consistently throughout the novel, although the two never marry or remain faithful to one another. He meets her when she is only 18 and mourning for two lovers killed in an accident at the railroad tracks (reminiscent of the heroine in Hannah's story "Coming Close to Donna" in *Airships*). Her deep-skinned, Cajun beauty and her truthful attitude toward life convince Ray that love and hope are indeed possible in a world devoid of meaning and real affection: "I don't feel that good about women anyway, nor gooks, nor sand-niggers, nor doctors, nor anything human that moves, with its zealous raving habits. Then I met Sister and my trust came back, my body was flooded with hope" (*Ray,* 10). Although their relationship is almost a purely sexual one, Ray finds Sister more appealing than either of his wives; married or single, he remains unable to resist Sister's charm. He pays for her to attend the University of South Alabama in Mobile, and after she drops out, he rushes to meet her in Atlanta when marijuana and prostitution threaten to destroy her sense of well-being. Their relationship represents Ray's possibilities of redemption through love, but he never commits himself fully to her before she is murdered by a hypocritical preacher, Maynard Castro, who both appreciates and criticizes her promiscuity.

For a short time Ray finds a similar hope in the arms of his second wife, Westy: "Westy has an uncommon adventurous warmth to her, a crazy hope in her blue eyes, and a body that will keep a lover occupied. I was gone for her about first sight" (*Ray,* 31). Ray sees in Westy and her two children a more ordered and supportive life for himself and his three children from his previous marriage than he could ever experience with Sister, and he relies on her quiet strength and unselfish love: "Westy does not talk much about the act of love. She just does it with all her heart" (*Ray*, 33). But, as Ray admits to himself and his audience, his tendency to value "fucking" above commitment disrupts any real hope of marital or familial bliss. He only remains faithful to his first wife when he is in Saigon because of the possibility of catching venereal disease and an unrequited love for the serene and beautiful Colonel's wife. With Westy, he is not so strong.

Although Ray tries to convince himself that adultery would interrupt and possible permanently prevent the type of life-style he envisions with Westy, his endeavors to stop himself from cheating with other women prove fruitless:

But this lowly barnacle of unfaithfulness would not leave my mind. It is enough to be married to a good woman. It is plenty.

Ray, the filthy call of random sex is a killer. It kills all you know of the benevolent order of your new life. (*Ray*, 37)

Ray tries to convince himself as well as the audience that nothing equals marriage to the right woman, but he remains unable to control his need for illicit excitement and passion: "Sister. Listen. I want you. My beloved wife does not seem awfully inspired in the bedroom lately" (*Ray*, 47). When Westy leaves him and Sister is killed in a freak accident, Ray finds himself alone with his son Barry and his daughter Lee. Her possible pregnancy at 42 reconciles Westy with Ray temporarily, but the death of this dream ultimately prevents the couple's reunion. Like Harriman Monroe in *Geronimo Rex*, Ray needs more sex and music; a marriage to one woman cannot satisfy his insatiable desires.

Ray's three preoccupations—healing, flying, and fucking—are self-serving and egotistical. But Hannah introduces a side to Ray that the character neither acknowledges nor uses to manipulate readers—that of the artist and philosopher. The rare moments when Ray cares more about others than himself reveal aspects of the character that, although they do not excuse his selfishness and violence, make him seem substantial and worthy of concern. During one of his many reconciliations with Westy, for example, Ray dreams of utopia: "I'm dreaming of the day when the Big C [cancer] will be blown away. I'm dreaming of a world where men and women have stopped the war and where we will stroll as naked excellent couples under the eye of the sweet Lord again. I'm dreaming of the children whom I have hurt from being hurt and the hurt they learn, the cynicism, the precocious wit, the poo-poo, the slanted mouth, the supercilious eyebrow" (*Ray*, 82).

When he awakens to Westy's accusation that he has been dreaming of "some patient he screwed," Ray chooses not to defend himself. He understands that her accusations are rooted in his external behavior, but he confesses quietly to his readers that "between the lines I'm looking for the cure for cancer" (*Ray*, 83). It is this gray area "between the lines" that Hannah uses to earn respect for his protagonist.

Ray's appreciation for Mr. Hooch's uncanny ability to write poetry also illustrates that he is interested in building more than just his own ego. Although he is jealous of Hooch's ability to capture life through poetic form, he admires his friend's insight: "He's beating the shit out of Shakespeare with his new ones" (*Ray*, 96). Humiliated by his emotional response to Hooch's poem about his dead daughter, Ray hides in the bathroom to cry privately. His reaction to Hooch's poetry illustrates that not only is Ray able to appreciate the beauty of true art, but that he is also able to fear more deeply than his concerns with macho appearances and brute strength will allow him to express. His prayer for his stepson, that the boy will travel with beauty and that he will "never be cruel, weird, or abusive," reveals his hope that his loved ones will overcome his own fears and prejudices (*Ray*, 91). And, in spite of his behavior toward Westy, readers believe that Ray actually loves her and sees in her hope for the future. Ray may indeed be weak, pompous, and selfish, but Hannah encourages readers to understand that his true worth lies in his private dreams and hidden emotional reactions.

The ending of the novel emphasizes this side of Ray. As the novel progresses, the chapters grow shorter and the pace quickens. Hannah attributes the brevity and disjunctiveness of *Ray* to his own life at the time: "It came out of a period of agony and drunken angst, and it was better to make it short and sweet than just to babble or tell some cranked up Southern story again" (Vanarsdall, 322). Hannah understands that as the length of the fragments decreases, "Ray is getting more frantic. His concentration is going . . . becoming more desperate . . . it's getting difficult for him to speak" (Vanarsdall, 339). But he hopes, as the chapters become more fragmented, the ideas grow more crystalline. The more segmented the novel becomes, the more the thoughtful side of Ray emerges, that which hopes for a cure for cancer and expresses concern for his family. Hannah wants his readers to recognize that Ray, unlike himself, is a doctor, not a writer (although Hannah did attend medical school briefly): "He's lumbering between banality and some gripping thought, and he's trying. But he doesn't probably have the natural thing. He keeps at it, though, which is important" (Vanarsdall, 339).

The last chapter of the novel, section 62, ties these ideas together in a conclusion that is both encouraging and optimistic. Not only is Ray's own poetry improving, which illustrates a sharpened perception and a commitment to art, but he is also at least temporarily reunited with Westy, sexually *and* emotionally. His pal Charlie de Soto is reconciled with his wife Eileen, and even his nurses are getting married. Ray finds that the ordinary now brings delight instead of despair: "The Alabama team is still whipping everybody in sight. My patients are calling. Bill is getting ready to fight. Elizabeth is looking in the Holy Bible. Mr. Hooch has his hands on a pencil" (*Ray*, 113). This appreciation of the smaller triumphs satisfies Ray, at least for an afternoon, and it also distances him from his all-encompassing self-concern. As Donald R. Noble writes, "So Hannah is not a nihilist. He is aware of the pain in life, of the terrible potential for pain that is inherent in loving, but his characters keep trying" (*Southern Literary Journal,* 44). Ray is aware of this pain, and even the extent to which he is responsible, but at the end of the novel he temporarily absolves himself and those around him from blame to enjoy the possibilities that life offers. When, in the last line of the novel, Ray proclaims "Sabers, gentlemen, sabers!," he acknowledges that although his dream of utopia is unlikely, ideals of honor, gentility, and sacrifice can be maintained in the midst of a life that is primarily painful. From the hospital to the hearth, Ray finds, after expressing the fragments that make up his life, that his real pleasures lie not in healing, flying, and fucking; rather, he discovers that commitment, family, and friendship potentially reap more substantial rewards.

The Tennis Handsome: The Conflict between the Physical and the Intellectual

Like *Ray, The Tennis Handsome* also disjoints conventional chronology and linear plot in favor of a plotless, fragmented narrative. *The Tennis Handsome,* however, offers a variety of characters each with different perspectives, from Baby Levaster, who cares for and thinks for French Edward, the tennis pro of the title, to Bobby Smith, the Vietnam veteran who is forced to readapt to civilian life. The first two chapters of the novel, fully one-third of the book, Hannah borrows almost directly from two stories in *Airships.* Although he slightly alters the stories to make the novel more coherent, the primary factor unifying the characters' stories, especially early in the novel, is their mutual birthplace: Vicksburg, Mississippi. "Return to Return," the first chapter in *The Tennis Handsome,* provides the exposition that binds the lives of Levaster, Word, and Edward together. It describes in third person the obsession of Baby Levaster, Tulane M.D., and Dr. James Word, his high school tennis coach, with the charismatic tennis player, French Edward; both men use Edward to compensate for their own physical inadequacies. Baby Levaster, who met French Edward in high school, has become a doctor who hates the sight of pain and blood: "by this time he had become a weak, balding drunkard of a very disagreeable character, even to himself. He dragged himself from one peak of cowardice to the next."[8] In Edward, Levaster envies the physical potential he never attained: "He had never seen anything so handsome as this French Edward. . . . Baby Levaster had the distinct sensation that his heart had settled into the breast of French Edward. He saw a man who moved as if animal secrets were known to him" (*TH*, 14).

Dr. Word, Levaster and Edward's tennis coach in high school, also admires Edward's physical prowess and beauty. Although Word is responsible for Edward's success, his homosexual advances repulse Edward: "He had never liked Dr. Word, even as he had learned from him. He had never liked the man's closeness. . . . For instance, Word would every now and then give him a *pinch*, a hard affectionate little nip of the fingers" (*TH*, 11). When Word falls in love with French Edward's mother Olive at first sight, he abandons his homosexual inclinations and fosters between them a torrid sexual affair, which French witnesses. To exact revenge, Edward maneuvers a tennis match between himself and his 60-year-old coach, hoping to kill his mother's lover; instead, Word lives but is partially disabled from a stroke brought on by Edward's physical challenge: "Word's arm was still curled up with stroke, and he had only a sort of quarter vision in one eye. His voice was frightful, like that of a man in a cave of wasps" (*TH*, 13). French Edward not only fails to prevent Word from continuing his illicit relationship with Olive, but he is also unable to stop Word from following his tennis career. When Word almost drowns, Edward, in an effort to prevent Word's suicide attempt, falls 200 feet in the river with him: "He had drowned and had broken one leg, but had crawled out of the water anyhow. His brain was damaged" (*TH*, 36). Levaster, seizing his opportunity, fulfills his fantasy to join his mind with Edward's body: "Levaster's body fled away from his bones and gathered onto the muscles of French Edward, as if his poor sinews had surrounded French as a kind of halo" (*TH*, 22). Much of *The Tennis Handsome* chronicles the further adventures of Levaster, who thinks *for* French Edward, and Word, who thinks only *of* him.

The second chapter, "Midnight and I'm Not Famous Yet," retells the story of Bobby Smith from *Airships,* the virgin soldier in Vietnam forced to kill the captured Vietnam general Li Dap, who bases much of his military strategy on the history of Jeb Stuart: "He knows Robert Lee and the strategy of J. E. B. Stuart, whose daring circles around an immense army captured his mind. Li Dap wants to be J. E. B. Stuart" (*TH*, 44). When his photographer friend from Virginia, Ike "Tubby" Wooten, is killed in a freak accident in Vietnam, Smith hopes to use Tubby's pictures to make his dead friend famous, but the Pentagon confiscates the pictures and Wooten's superior photographic ability goes unrecognized. A cynical and dissatisfied civilian after the war, Smith loses his virginity and with it his sense of self-worth: "Since I've been home I've got in bed with almost anything that would have me. I've slept with my old high school teachers, with Negroes, and the other night, with my own aunt" (*TH*, 51). During and after the war, only the stories of French Edward give Smith faith in himself and his country: "It made me love America, to know he was in it. . . . The way French Edward looked, it sort of rebuked yourself ever hoping to call yourself a man" (*TH*, 41–42). In the remaining 16 chapters of *The Tennis Handsome*, Hannah juxtaposes achronologically the stories of Smith, Levaster, Word, and their friends and relatives using Edward's physical beauty to bind the characters together.

The Tennis Handsome met with milder critical reception than either *Airships* or *Ray*, but most of the reviews were positive. Although *New Republic* reviewer Jack Beatty wrote that in Hannah's fifth book, "There is no plot, no unfolding logic of development, no growth of character,"[9] Ivan Gold of the *New York Times Book Review* appreciated Hannah's unusual perspective: "There is endless instruction and delight in watching him refine his idiosyncratic vision, chipping away at the block of marble, fashioning a Yoknapatawpha County of the mind."[10] But Gold tired of the countless comparisons critics make between Hannah, Welty, Faulkner, and O'Connor: "He is an original, or if names are to be dropped, Carson McCullers rewritten by Groucho Marx" (Gold, 19). *Booklist* wrote that Hannah's "verbal sleights of hand and satire are served up deliciously,"[11] and *Time* praised Hannah's style and wit: "The true star is Hannah's protean comic prose. He can deadpan with the best of them."[12] Most critics noted the plotlessness of *The Tennis Handsome*, but only Jack Beatty and Christopher Lehmann-Haupt believed that its disjunctive nature lessened its effectiveness.[13]

And, indeed, the humor and insight Hannah achieves in *The Tennis Handsome* relies on its fragmented style and intentional lack of continuity. In his fourth novel Hannah depends more heavily on a sense of the grotesque than in his previous novels. Word continues to survive despite his stroke and suicide attempt; Edward regains some of his intelligence and a

penchant for writing scatological verse when he is struck by lightning;
Smith has a sexual relationship with his aunt; and his aunt is almost raped
by a walrus. Hannah intends for his readers neither to believe the incidents
he describes nor to concern themselves with their chronology. Because the
characters in *The Tennis Handsome* are very much a product of their past
and present experiences, Hannah's random juxtaposition of events offers
psychological insight into their motivation.

For example, chapter 3, "His March through Time," describes the relationship between Word, his college roommate, Thorny, and Tyrone
Hibatchi, a Japanese prisoner who escaped from an internment camp after
the Japanese bombed Pearl Harbor. Although the information Hannah presents occurs before the story described in the first two chapters, Hannah
chooses not to present Word's story as a flashback. The reader understands
not only that Word's past affects his obsessive behavior in the present, but
also that linear time is almost a false construction when detailing memory.
Word loses Thorny to a bomber in South America, and Tyrone to a suicide
attempt prompted by Word's inadequacies as a researcher and friend.
Through these two losses, Word learns that he must accept himself as he is:
"When they come, there will be no apologies, thought Word. All of this is
me. This is what Word thought to himself, and then he rushed to comfort
Tyrone's head" (*TH*, 69). The realization of his own inadequacies leads
Word to depend too heavily on furthering his relationship with Olive and
her son. In spite of the physical and emotional hardships these dependencies
cause, Word is not strong enough to abandon either, even for his own good.
Hannah juxtaposes the story of Word's past between the tale of Bobby
Smith in Vietnam and French's encounter with the bolt of lightning to explain Word's interest in the Edward family and to build upon the idea that
loss in *The Tennis Handsome* inspires characters to choose desperate and destructive paths.

Often in *The Tennis Handsome* Hannah juxtaposes events to disrupt the
narrative even further, purposely confusing the reader. In the chapter following Elizabeth's abandonment of her nephew Bobby ("The Physician
Touches a Delicate Heart"), Hannah describes the adventures of a half-
Choctaw woman who lives on a houseboat with her sons and a mysterious
older man the family has saved. Within the course of the chapter readers
discover that this mysterious man is Dr. James Word, but until then,
Hannah uses titles and vague pronoun references to hide the identity of his
characters from the readers: "The old man was in the bow of the boat. . . .
he was frozen on beer, leaning over the rail in the image of a sex-ridden
mourner. . . . The woman was in the kitchen, cleaning a duck shot out of

season" (*TH*, 92–93). This intentional dislocation of character, time, and space distances readers from the narrative, a Brechtian device, in order to regain perspective and clarify intention. Hannah admitted to Vanarsdall that his narrative style is difficult to comprehend, but he feels ultimately that it illustrates faith in his readers: "I treat my readers better than a lot of writers do. I expect a hip, wise reader. . . . I expect some complicity with it. I hope I can get this. We're in this together and I'm writing the best I can" (Vanarsdall, 340). In *The Tennis Handsome* Hannah challenges readers to look beyond the narrative to recognize associations between juxtaposed prose passages. Characters, then, are defined not only by their own stories, but also by their placement within an achronological structure.

Hannah uses this form of narrative partially to imitate the power memory has to direct the lives of three of his protagonists: Baby Levaster, James Word, and Bobby Smith. None of them wishes to reexamine the past, but each is unable to escape the powerful influence of memory. Before French's tennis match with V. T. in Boston, for example, Levaster's memories interfere with his present: "Levaster's mind fled to a summer during his college days when he had worked at a camp for retarded children in Louisiana. It was French's mention of the shoes from Sears that had taken his mind back to the fenced recreation lot" (*TH*, 72). And when Word lives on the Choctaw woman's houseboat, he also tries to avoid the past: "Word's memory erupted with an agony. But he did not want to think of the past. And so it seemed the past was thinking of him" (*TH*, 94). The past drags Word almost unwillingly into memories of his job as an official in the Fish and Game Department, his first pistol, and his violent encounter with a midget arsonist. And Bobby Smith recounts in first person the difficulties of escaping the past to proceed with the present: "I have my own stadium of the dead around me. Out in the field is Tubby and the took [captured] general. They're out there all the time, winning and losing" (*TH*, 110). Hannah's characters in *The Tennis Handsome* are more than products of the past: they remain its prisoner, constantly entrapped within their individual "stadium of the dead." Because none of them chooses to share these memories with others, real communication becomes impossible, and characters feel as if they have no power over their destinies. Controlling French Edward's future, then, takes on added significance for all three men. If the lives of Levaster, Word, and Smith ultimately lack purpose or direction, at least their ability to influence Edward implies a causal force on the universe.

For Levaster, Edward provides a reason to continue living. Failed relationships, a failed marriage, and a failed career lead Levaster back to Edward: "Some years passed and Levaster was forty. He opened the clinic in

New Orleans again. Then he closed it and returned to New York. Now he admitted that he languished when French Edward was out of his vision. A hollow inconsequence filled his acts, good or evil, whenever French was not near" (*TH,* 31). French's near-drowning is a blessing for Levaster, who sees Edward's crippled mind as providing for him a reason to live. He abandons his profession and his wife Louise, not to take care of Edward, but to give his life a sense of purpose. He agrees to marry the deformed Inez because she bears French's child, and he initiates an affair with Olive Edward more to possess the son than the mother. But partially inspired by the obsessive need for French, Levaster drives himself toward his own destruction. He promises too much to too many: "The whole place seems made of demands" (*TH,* 119). Although he finally marries the crippled Inez, thereby committing bigamy, she dies on the operating table, leaving Levaster in charge of Edward's daughter, Murphy. When French and Levaster argue over custody of the child and French's ensuing independence, Cecilia, French's wife, murders Levaster with a crossbow. Hannah makes it clear that Levaster's death is no tragedy; without French's mind or child to control, Levaster sees no purpose in life. His death, ironically, is a blessing.

In spite of Edward's hatred for him, Word also views the tennis pro as a reason to continue living. Like Levaster, he unsuccessfully tries to possess both the boy and his mother. Word not only calls Edward his son, but he also refuses to admit that his compulsion to follow French's career psychologically torments the tennis player. Consistently meeting with Edward's disapproval, Word begins to lose his reason. He is arrested for serving tennis balls inside a department store, and when he attempts to find Olive for salvation, he discovers her in bed with Baby Levaster: "Word puked bile and tracked it on the rug. The world cracked around him, crowded and loud. . . . Why, why, why, why don't I die?" (*TH,* 103). Saved by Smith, Word desperately follows Edward to New Orleans to observe his match against Billy Devis from Southern California. After watching Edward beat Devis, Word dies peacefully in Smith's car. The coach's inability to continue to affect the lives of either Olive or French literally kills him. Ironically, his corpse, dumped into the Mississippi River by Smith, exhibits more life and independence than Word does when alive: "Word slept with the fish. Like them, he made friends with the continental sewage of the Mississippi. . . . Word was making fast time. In a week, he would be at the Three Fingers Saloon" (*TH,* 133). Like Levaster, Word seems more satisfied dead than alive.

Although Captain Bobby Smith's story is the only one recounted in first person, his obsession for French is more difficult to understand than

Levaster's or Word's. Unable to live with the murders he committed in Vietnam, Smith turns to his Aunt Elizabeth for forgiveness and salvation. When she leaves him, his idolatry for Edward increases. He not only admires the tennis player's extraordinary physical grace, but he appreciates that an athletic match offers players an opportunity to do battle with no real losses: "Nobody was killed! We saw victory and defeat and they were both wonderful" (*TH*, 51). He travels with Levaster and French to avoid his fear of loneliness, memories, and home. He takes in Word primarily to absolve himself from his guilt over deaths in Vietnam: "It was Captain Bob Smith, crazy to preserve people and make up for some dead men" (*TH*, 112). After Word's death, Smith attempts a reconciliation with his Aunt Beth, but she leaves him when he murders a walrus that attempts to rape her. Left alone, he watches another Edward tennis match, lives for a while with Levaster and Murphy, and is abandoned by them at the end of the novel, leaving him alone and unhappy: "But they were gone. They were entirely gone out of the house. He looked in the yard. He looked in the overgrown grass. He dug down into the litter" (*TH*, 156). Hannah never mentions Smith again; without some association with Edward or the people around him, Smith loses his purpose and identity as a character. He never learns that people cannot absolve themselves from past deeds; he must find the strength to forgive himself.

Although he is the central character in *The Tennis Handsome*, French Edward has less identity than any of the other figures in the novel. Even as a child, he goes unnoticed by his mother and father. During his mother's affair with Dr. Word, he remains almost invisible under their bed listening: "So he crawled under the bed of his room and slept so as to gather the episode into a dream" (*TH*, 10). He attempts ineffectually to rid his mother of Dr. Word, and he marries Cecilia more from obligation than love. Although his near-drowning increases French's dependence on Levaster, the tennis player is unable to think for himself even before the accident: "Don't leave me Baby. I need your mind with me. Somebody from Vicksburg. Somebody who knows" (*TH*, 16). The accident, ironically, only strengthens his physical prowess; he wins more easily without thinking than he did when his mind worked normally. Those around him, from his wife to his mentor, may use him to achieve self-gratification, but Edward never seems to recognize the need he fulfills in them. For the first half of the novel, he is a comic parody of the true athlete: unthinking, unfeeling, unargumentative, and uninteresting. In Boston, however, when French is struck by lightning, he regains some of the knowledge lost in the river, and with it, independence. Although he ultimately agrees to Levaster's demand that he continue the match, he argues for the first time: " 'Hey!' said French Edward. 'I know my own self ' " (*TH,* 76). French's clearer vision initiates the first argument between the two men, prompting Levaster's temporary desertion. When Baby returns, Edwards is not only winning, but he is also inspired by the muse of poetry.

Unfortunately, the effect of the lightning is only temporary; as Edward continues to travel he regresses to his former, unbalanced state. To recover, he becomes an electricity addict, and he asks Bobby Smith to help him find an electricity "fix": "I wish you could score some electricity for me tonight. . . . We could buy some jumper cables and go down to the Greyhound station. I could stand in water" (*TH,* 150). Edward's obsessive need for electricity reflects his desire to be independent of others and to think for himself. He may essentially be the pawn of each character in the novel, but at the end he is the sole character who manages to find happiness and to build a life for his family. Not only does he reclaim his daughter from Levaster, but he begins to meet with widespread critical acclaim for his quatrains. Although he eventually loses any sense of reality, French survives in *The Tennis Handsome:* "Ideas tended to stand around in his head like gray animals of no intent, neither coming nor going. Every now and then something larger than the others lay back as if to fly off, and this caused the soles of his feet to itch" (*TH,* 162). As he watches his son play tennis, he thinks of Olive, Word, and redemption. His final celestial images, Olive chewing a transubstantiation wafer, his son playing tennis beyond the capabilities of Jesus, and the power and influence of music, suggest that Edward's madness is no longer abused by others; rather, he finds himself in his own self-created state of grace.

As in his previous fiction, Hannah uses violence as a means of expression shared by each of the characters, but in *The Tennis Handsome,* the violence is as confusing and random as the book's narrative structure. Levaster, like Ray, enjoys the thought of violence, and appreciates New York primarily because of the city's resemblance to the wilderness of Vicksburg (where he once enjoyed hunting): "But he assumed this New York thing to be more sporting, walking along in the filthy reality of the metropolis as bait for the muggers, who might have their own pistols, etc. Who knows what marvels of violence would ensue?" (*TH,* 7). Like a hunter, Levaster baits his prey in Central Park. He takes his girlfriend Carina there, hoping to tempt potential bums and rapists. When they do appear he feigns weakness and then uses his concealed gun to attack the would-be accosters. He attempts to choke a fan who does not like French Edward, and carries a .40 pistol to shoot a Cuban who makes a rude gesture. Levaster enjoys the "sport" of hunting, but he must possess an unfair advantage, such as a concealed weapon, to win. His death by crossbow ironically makes Levaster the hunted, and because Cecilia takes him by surprise, he falls as easily as the prey he stalked during his life.

If Levaster is the hunter in *The Tennis Handsome,* then Word is the hunted, a victim of others' needs for violence. Hoping to kill his mother's lover, French challenges the 60-year-old Word to a tennis match on the second-hottest day of the year: "French had him fooled. He pretended to fail in the heat, knocking slow balls from corner to corner, easing over a drop shot to watch the old man go mad to get it. . . . it wasn't long before the old devil keeled over, falling out in the alley with his raquet clattering. . . . French was hoping for a heart attack" (*TH,* 12). Although Word attempts to avoid confrontations with violence, those around him succumb to violent influences. His lover Thorny, a navigator, dies when he is attacked by a bomber on his way to the African front, and his Japanese friend Tyrone plants a butcher knife in his own belly, attempting unsuccessfully to commit suicide. Incidents like these destroy Word's trust in others and in himself. He grows increasingly frightened of loss and physical attack. For example, when he is attacked by cashiers in an economy mart, Word vomits and expels gas, and when he finds Olive with Levaster, he would rather die than confront the woman who has betrayed him. Even after Word dies, Smith's wish for the tennis coach is violent: "I waited till I heard the splash, and then I prayed to the river. 'Take care of him. Take him under and tear him apart' " (*TH,* 132).

Violence also destroys Bobby Smith, the most peace-loving character in *The Tennis Handsome.* His success in Vietnam makes him a victim of his own deeds and actions. Fear inspires Bobby to excel as a soldier in Vietnam. He kills to protect himself: "If you ever hear one bullet pass you, you get sick thinking there might be hundreds of them. All you can do is point your gun down and shoot it out" (*TH,* 42). Smith commands respect from his troops, primarily because he kills gooks, but in Vietnam he hides from his men his true feelings about the murders he commits: "I started crying. It came on me with these hard sobs jamming up like rocks in my throat" (*TH,* 47). Only the image of French Edward preserves him, a symbol of violence without death: "The picture of French Edward about to hit that ball at Forest Hills was stuck in my head. There was such care in his eyes, and it was only a tennis ball, a goddamned piece of store-bought bounce. But it was wonderful and nobody was being killed. The tears were out on my jaws then. Here we shot each other up" (*TH,* 47). After Tubby's death, Smith reacts without thinking. He aims his bayonet and shoots uncontrollably, killing captured general Li Dap and at least 20 Vietnamese. As a civilian after the war, he tries unsuccessfully to prevent the deaths of others, from James Word to Baby Levaster, partially to redeem himself from his previous actions. He discovers, however, that the present can never excuse the past. Smith is doomed to a life of haunting memories and violent dreams. Hannah gives Smith a moral consciousness lacking in characters such as Harriman Monroe and Ray. Only Smith in *The Tennis Handsome* understands the paradoxical power of violence to control and to destroy.

Hannah's vision in *The Tennis Handsome* is ultimately more comical and satirical than violent. Unlike *Ray,* which was written after one of Hannah's difficult divorces, *The Tennis Handsome* was originally supposed to be a nonfiction tennis book for Lippincott. Hannah explained to Vanarsdall the origins of the novel: "My tennis player, Bob Lutz, broke his leg on the tour. . . . I also found out that tennis players are dull, and I didn't want to write a non-fiction book. . . . So I came home and invented my own tennis player" (Vanarsdall, 323–24). The novel satirizes the emphasis Americans place on athletics; the violence comically explores in depth the psychological makeup of three men who idolize tennis for different reasons. Like Harriman, Thorpe, and Ray, Levaster, Word, and Smith search desperately for salvation. In the persona of French Edward they discover, if only momentarily, some method to allow them to escape from their own existence. Whereas Ray justifiably and unjustifiably finds heroism within his own actions, Levaster, Word, and Smith are unable to locate within their memories of the past and present any feasible explanation for their existence. Crosscutting between these three protagonists, Hannah creates a grotesque universe of characters who look to tennis and Edward for salvation. None of them finds it, however, because each remains unable to face or understand the consequences of his past, but the problems they encounter in their journey for redemption are both humorous and touching.

Hannah's sense of the ludicrous in *The Tennis Handsome* helps to create comedy in the midst of pathos and, at the same time, illustrates his ability to write original prose. For example, when Levaster marries Louise, his mother attends the wedding: "Levaster's mother came too, talking about the weather and her new shoes. Someone mistook her for nothing in one of the chairs and sat on her" (*TH,* 26). This sense of absurdity Hannah carries throughout *The Tennis Handsome,* often using it to define character flaws or describe emotional problems. As Word harbors Tyrone, Hannah recounts in grotesquely exaggerated terms the Japanese man's increasing problems with weight control:

Tyrone's eyes could barely be seen anymore. They were swine's eyes. He ate steak, chicken, gravy, rolls, fried catfish, and took down the butter neat. . . . His bottom was more than a yard wide. A rim of grease lay around his lips. This is revenge, some order of revenge on some order of something, thought Word.

He had seen Tyrone pour cooking oil over a loaf of white bread, pepper the thing lustily, then eat it. (*TH,* 66)

Hannah humorously exaggerates to distance readers from the pathos of Tyrone's loneliness and inability to control the American penchant for excess; at the same time, Tyrone's eventual suicide attempt illustrates that Hannah does not mean for readers to ignore the seriousness behind the comedy. He may frame an incident within the absurd, but his satirical edge forces readers to face the serious consequences of a world with misplaced values and confused ethics.

For example, in the midst of Hannah's most humorous passages, he satirizes prejudice, adolescence, and sports. The store manager who throws Word from the economy mart is "a big-breasted solemnity with frozen tall hydra curls, talented at being curt to poor white trash as only poor white trash itself can be" (*TH,* 100). A high school band singer is described as a "wretched pubescent with dingy chin-hairs," and French's brother Jubal, at five years old, is killed running for a football: "Had him going out for a pass in the front yard and the sucker went over him, so he chased it, by God. Out on into the street and a big Buick tackled the little fellow. Now *that's* what I call hustle" (*TH,* 109). Even French's poetry represents Hannah's ability to combine the grotesque with the satirical:

> It does not make a damn who wins this game,
> It does not mean one twit who loses
>   Except to loud and empty shits
> And fuck-ups and dumb-fucks and cocksuckers.
>   (*TH,* 109)

Although the poem comically fails as art, it succeeds in concretizing one of the novel's messages: that Hannah's characters look to sports as a microcosm of success. Winning may be all-important to Levaster, Word, and Edward, but this drive to succeed at all costs is ultimately destructive. Ironically, only French, the least "normal" character in the novel, is capable of seeing past the superficial aspects of tennis and life.

Hannah's vision in *The Tennis Handsome,* in spite of his satirical edge, is ultimately less bleak than that reflected in his previous novels. As in

Geronimo Rex, Nightwatchmen, and *Ray,* he ends *The Tennis Handsome* with
hope for a better life in future generations. The final chapter, "Furtherance,"
describes what becomes of French and Inez's daughter, Murphy. She graduates from L.S.U.N.O., marries a nice fellow named Barry who has a passion
for tennis, and is happy: "But Murphy stayed cheerful enough, and her
cheer made Barry very happy. They were really a good, an abiding, an aver-
age American couple" (*TH,* 165). Although she cares for tennis much less
than her husband, Murphy enjoys watching him lose:

> It made her heart call out to see it. It didn't matter that he was her man. It wasn't
> taking sides or that brand of thing. It was something else, and it made, just for the
> instant, her heart sing.
>   Like this.
>   *Hit it. Hit, hit, my life, hit.* (*TH,* 166).

Like her adopted father, Baby Levaster, Murphy sees something magical in
the game of tennis, but, unlike Levaster, Murphy finds within herself—and
not tennis—the strength and satisfaction to make living purposeful and
significant.

   Hannah fragments *The Tennis Handsome* for many of the same reasons
he breaks *Ray* into blocks of disjointed narrative. Such a structure allows
him the freedom to imitate the thought processes of the characters in his
novels, while simultaneously satirizing their inability to make sense of life.
The technique is, on the one hand, realistic, and, on the other, grotesquely
comic. In *Ray* and *The Tennis Handsome* he pulls farther away from the bildungsroman form of *Geronimo Rex* and the heavily plotted *Nightwatchmen.*
Influenced by his success with the stories in *Airships,* Hannah shortens the
length of his fiction, lessens his emphasis on plot, and begins to break down
temporal and spatial restrictions. His narrative may confuse his readers, but
it manages to describe in original terms the struggles his protagonists have
in learning to understand, love, and appreciate themselves. Hannah's fragmented structure realistically imitates lives that are no longer explained or
defended in terms of straightforward causal relationships. In *The Tennis
Handsome* and *Ray* Hannah aims at uncovering the comedy and pathos of
the minds of his characters. Memory takes precedence over action, and plot
is subordinated to the complexity and insight of the thought process.

Chapter Four

"A Certain Peace": The Movement toward Resolution in *Captain Maximus*

Barry Hannah's second collection of short stories, *Captain Maximus* (1985), disappointed critics such as Terrence Rafferty of the *Nation,* who advised Hannah to "cut out the voodoo and try speaking to us again in the expansive, outgoing novelist's voice of *Geronimo Rex,*"[1] and James Wolcott of the *New York Review of Books* who observed, "Frequently Hannah seems less interested in telling a tale than in embellishing a reputation as demon drinker and campus tongue."[2]

Consisting of seven stories and an extended "screenplay-story" written for director Robert Altman, *Captain Maximus* is indeed a thinner and less ambitious work than the earlier *Airships,* but it reflects a significant transition for Hannah both in terms of style and theme. Although only the final story in the collection, "Power and Light," is subtitled "an idea for film," Hannah's style throughout many of the stories in *Captain Maximus* shares cinematic techniques that resemble montage. His stories continue to present malcontent drifters straining for self-understanding and growth, but now Hannah describes their tales by splicing together moments of their life without adhering to either traditional chronology of time or unity of place. Ironically, Hannah uses this violent and disruptive cinematic technique to carry his *Captain Maximus* narrators further than characters from his previous fiction; like Maximus Ned in the story "Ride, Fly, Penetrate, Loiter," many of the central figures in *Captain Maximus* discover the pleasure and paradoxes of reaching "a certain peace."

Autobiographical Tales: Life after Violence

The first seven stories in *Captain Maximus* present autobiographical matter familiar to readers of Hannah's earlier fiction. They still involve his narrators in drunken brawls, tall tales, plane crashes, and practical jokes, but, unlike the stories in *Airships,* most end with characters at least reaching a satisfactory compromise, if not discovering a peaceable resolution. Hannah experiments with first-, second-, and third-person narration, binding readers to the narrators while simultaneously pushing them away. As in *Ray,* Hannah in *Captain Maximus* acknowledges his audience, but the tone is more subdued now than playful, more ambiguous than absurd. James Wolcott, in his article "Southern Discomfort," wrote that in the new collection of short stories, "Hannah is carrying a more mellow tune" (Wolcott, 33), while Christopher Lehmann-Haupt agreed in his *New York Times* review that "Hannah seems to be calming down a little. . . . His people seem ready for simpler resolutions than in his previous work."[3] In *Captain Maximus* Hannah continues to elaborate upon man's destructive impulses toward his fellow man and himself, but violence is rarely adopted as the primary solution to problems with relationships or self-image. Instead, Hannah's narrators in *Captain Maximus* represent life after violence; they struggle to find satisfaction in a world that seems to enjoy denying it.

Although each of the seven stories that precede "Power and Light" describes narrators in similarly confusing and obsessive situations, three of the short stories, "Getting Ready," "Even Greenland," and "Fans," present their protagonists' dilemmas in straightforward and chronological narrative form. The strength of each story lies not in the originality of Hannah's characters or the experimental structure of the works; rather, the power of the three tales depends on the irony of their conclusions, which illustrates that only by sacrificing societal ties and individual freedom can protagonists obtain their elusive goals. The first story in the collection, "Getting Ready," tells of Roger Laird, a 48-year-old fisherman who, in spite of repeated efforts and great expense, "had never caught a significant fish."[4] An avid reader of *Fish & Stream* and a regular viewer of Southern television shows about baiting hooks and evaluating rods, Laird's obsession with catching one huge fish has gradually emptied his bank account and weakened his family ties. In spite of his good looks and more-than-reasonable success with financial speculation, Roger judges himself entirely upon his inability to land a fish of significant proportions. He even compares himself unfavorably to the crab that he caught mistakenly on his line yesterday: "The crab was ageing well and, dumb as hell, was holding on till the very, very last, where Roger might drag him in out of the water if he wanted him" (*CM,* 7). At the end of the story, after a lifetime of failures as a fisherman, Roger, now in Mexico City, spies the big fin of his obsessions. In front of a crowd, Roger lands the 15-pound, four-foot-long sand shark, only to throw it back into the water. He returns home bankrupt but happier in his marriage, moves to an unknown address in Dallas, and yells obscenities from a pair of home-built stilts eight feet high at wealthy families who view sailing and fishing only as hobbies.

That Hannah's short tale of obsession playfully reminds readers of Hemingway's *The Old Man and the Sea* seems intentional. Protagonists in both works of fiction tie their sense of self-respect and identity to one goal, and both achieve these goals in the course of the stories only to discover that success does not bring about the changes they had desired. But Laird's search is literal rather than mythical; catching the fish represents an opportunity for him to prove his expertise to himself and to others. He is satisfied with the moderate-size sand shark because it completes his romantic perception of himself as a fisherman. The hostility he exhibits toward those wealthier and less obsessed fishermen at the end of the story paradoxically reflects both a satisfaction with deeds accomplished and a growing need to belittle others. In Laird's eyes, catching the sand shark makes him an authority and absolves him from his obsessive need to land another big fish; he is free to proceed with his life and marriage. But Hannah makes it clear at the end of the story that Laird's questionable success with fishing creates within him a need to distance himself from others. His feelings of superiority, encouraged by his success in obtaining his goal, separate him from the fishermen around him: "The sailing boats would come around near him, big opulent three-riggers sleeping two families below decks, and Roger Laird would yell, 'Fuck you! Fuck you!' " (*CM*, 16). Ironically, by fulfilling his desires, Laird loses the sense of individuality that comically defines him earlier in the story. In *Captain Maximus* narrators such as Roger achieve individuality only *during* their quests for self-fulfillment; *after* they achieve their goals they take their place in relative obscurity alongside a nation of others who lead normal but vacant lives. Roger resists this impulse at the end of the short story, but his gesture on the stilts reflects desperation and futility, not individuality.

The narrator in "Even Greenland," one of the shorter stories in *Captain Maximus,* shares Roger's dull, predictable existence. Even flying with fellow pilot and adventurer John affords him little excitement: "It doesn't matter after you've seen the curvature of the earth. For a while, nothing much matters at all. We'd had three sunsets already" (*CM*, 31). John, however, reveals that he is even less enthusiastic about life than the narrator, and when his plane catches fire he encourages his friend to save only himself. The narrator reluctantly ejects, leaving John to die in the plane crash. Years later, the narrator, now a lieutenant commander in the reserve, visits the site of the crash with his girl Celeste, and sits "absorbed and paralyzed" in front of John's "grave": "I know I am looking at John's damned triumph" (*CM*, 34).

In many respects, John's "suicide" parallels Roger's need to catch a significant fish. He confesses to his friend while the plane is on fire that "good" times—moments that combine physical excitement with purity of expression—are growing increasingly difficult to experience: "I haven't had a 'good time' in a long time. There's something between me and a good time since, I don't know, since I was twenty-eight or like that. I've seen a lot, but you know I haven't quite *seen* it. Like somebody's seen it already. It wasn't fresh. There were some eyes that had used it up some" (*CM*, 32). For John, even Greenland is ruined by footprints in the snow, indicating that nothing John sees or hears is pure, original, or untouched. When the narrator confesses to John that his one sacred memory is of snow in Mississippi, unencumbered by footsteps, he ironically seals John's fate: "You son of a bitch, that was *mine*—that snow in Mississippi. Now it's all shot to shit" (*CM*, 33). The only fresh, untouched, and completely personal act that John can experience is his own death, engineered by destiny but carried out intentionally. At the conclusion of the story the narrator is left as alienated as Roger in "Getting Ready." Although he has continued with his own life, as evidenced by his promotion and his girlfriend introduced at the end of the story, the narrator in "Even Greenland" is unable to react as he sits by his friend's crash site; he realizes that no future action that he performs will equal what he views as John's ultimate triumph of the will.

The third conventionally written story, "Fans," most resembles the stories from *Airships* that conclude violently and destructively. Written in third person, "Fans" describes the conversation between Wright's father, a sportswriter, and two of his drinking buddies—"Milton, who was actually blind but nevertheless a rabid fan, and Loomis Orange, the dwarf who was one of the team's managers" (*CM*, 55)—on the morning of the big football game in Oxford, Mississippi. Bar-talk turns to stories of J. Edward Toole, affectionally nicknamed "Jet," the Ole Miss defensive secondary and the team's star player, until Wright himself enters and recounts stories of his childhood friendship with the handsome hero. To his father's embarrassment, Wright repeats tales of incredible cruelty that Jet played upon him. The early pranks, from pinched breasts to accusations of flatulence, seem innocent enough, but the flood of memories reveals that Jet clipped Wright from behind on concrete floors, "clotheslined" him when he was riding his red Vespa motor scooter, and pushed him into shark-infested waters, resulting in Wright's "condition" and his dependence upon a walking cane. Only Wright sees irony in his final meeting with Jet on the Ole Mississippi campus: "I knew that he'd been born again and I wanted to congratulate him. You know what he said to me as he rubbed that big Sugar Bowl ring on that great sunbrowned finger of his? He put his arm on my shoulder and said to me, 'Wright, I'm sorry' " (*CM*, 60). In spite of Wright's story, however, and its implications, the four hobble out of the bar, meet Wright's mother, and head toward the stadium with the other fans "to wait for Jet to kill them" (*CM*, 60).

The atrocities that Wright recounts are new to no one in the bar; the friends of Wright's father have heard the "Jet" stories for years, and they enjoy reliving the violence almost as much as Wright enjoys telling them about it. Ironically, Wright's "condition" has also become his only ticket to local fame and immortality. He uses the shark story as an albatross around his neck, and appears whenever his father drinks before a game to garner sympathy and gain respect. Wright may not be Jet, but through sharing his childhood memories he becomes the next best thing: the man who was abused by the football hero. Wright's afflictions are analogous to John's intentional death in "Even Greenland." Both look at violence as a means to achieve self-worth and a moment of triumphant individuality, but whereas John destroys himself in one daring act of violent perfection, Wright lives to tell others of the cruel acts of violence that he has survived.

Even Wright's parents sacrifice their individuality to their son's tales of woe. Hannah never gives them names; instead, even among their friends they are referred to only as Wright's mother and father. Because they were unable to prevent Wright's harassment and suffering, they share in Jet's responsibility for his affliction and must pay by listening to him tell the story repeatedly. In "Fans" Hannah tears down the mythic ideal of the All-American football star, while satirizing those who blindly admire Jet for his Neanderthal ability to destroy the opponents of Ole Miss. The "fans" he refers to in the title appreciate more than just sporting events; Hannah writes of fans who also enjoy atrocities—from those drivers who slow down on the highway to catch a glimpse of the latest accident to the crowds who line up at fairs and circuses to laugh at freakish mistakes of nature. Hannah even aims "Fans" at readers of fiction, who, like Milton and Loomis Orange, take perverse delight in stories that end violently. Wright may join his parents and their friends at the Ole Miss game, but like Roger in "Getting Ready" and the narrator in "Even Greenland," his quest for individuality results in his inability to become one of the gang. Wright purposely uses his stories of Jet to set himself above the norm, ironically alienating himself from his family and friends.

In the four other stories in *Captain Maximus* preceding "Power and Light," Hannah abandons the reliance on conventional narrative form he uses in "Getting Ready," "Even Greenland," and "Fans" to recount autobiographical information in an almost cinematic structure. In "Idaho," "I Am Shaking to Death," "It Spoke of Exactly the Things," and especially "Ride, Fly, Penetrate, Loiter," Hannah creates a narrative structure that resembles montage, or associative editing, to juxtapose disjunctive and unrelated visual images. With these stories, Hannah joins twentieth-century *metafictionists* or *surfictionists,* postcontemporary authors who attempt to mirror the emotional disarray of societal transition. Raymond Federman, in his study of the postcontemporary novel, *Surfiction: Fiction Now . . . and Tomorrow,* adopts the term "surfiction" to define authors such as Hannah who write "that kind of fiction that tries to explore the possibilities of fiction; the kind of fiction that challenges the tradition that governs it; the kind of fiction that constantly renews our faith in man's imagination and not in man's distorted vision of reality—that reveals man's irrationality rather than man's rationality."[5] His initial article, "Surfiction—Four Propositions in Form of an Introduction," prescribes four significant characteristics of the postcontemporary movement to which Hannah subscribes in much of *Captain Maximus:*

1. *Novels must experiment with the printed word to redirect the method of reading.* Federman suggest transforming typography, syntax, and space to create a new form that challenges readers and forces their participation.

2. *Novels should overcome linear narration through exploring multiple and simultaneous attempts to rearrange material.* Only through rearranging narrative can surfictionists originate forms that mimic the chaotic movement of reality.

3. *Novels and characters should reflect authorial process and invention:* "The creatures of new fiction will be as changeable, as unstable, as illusionary, as nameless or unnameable, as fraudulent, as unpredictable as the discourse makes them" (Federman, 11–12).

4. *Fiction should offer no direct or complete meaning;* rather, "it will be deliberately illogical, irrational, unrealistic, non sequitur, and incoherent" (Federman, 11–12). Such apparently meaningless writing will force readers to determine thematic purpose through a more active exchange with the text itself.

Although one type of modern novel written by Hemingway, Faulkner, and Dos Passos experiments with multiperspectivism and juxtaposed forms, surfiction, for Federman, represents an even more intrinsic reader-participatory vehicle of self-knowledge and shared communication.

This postcontemporary emphasis on the "active exchange" between text and reader reflects the growing emphasis on the *process* of reading rather than on the novel as a finished, static product. The significance of characterization and plot diminishes, leaving the novel to investigate the elements of its own inception and generation. Ronald Sukenick's *In Form: Digressions on the Art of Fiction* provides one of the best descriptions and defenses of the subversiveness and disruption of modern fiction. Sukenick considers form "not a given but an object of invention . . . a dynamic, rather than an inert element of composition."[6] Surfictionists disrupt form by collage, fragmentation, extreme self-consciousness, self-reflexivity, discontinuity, surface artifice, increased visuals, and space/time experimentation to an unprecedented degree (Sukenick, 9–13). This disruption, according to Sukenick, ultimately makes the novel a viable structure; without it, "the form of the traditional novel is a metaphor for a society that no longer exists" (Sukenick, 3).

In "Idaho," Hannah's tribute to poet Richard Hugo and novelist Tom McGuane, he illustrates tendencies that Sukenick and Federman describe as postcontemporary, from the self-conscious, personal voice he chooses to narrate the story to the fragmented, juxtaposed "clumps" of narrative he uses to organize details. Although Hannah calls the story "Idaho," the narrator actually lives in Montana and teaches at the English Department in Missoula; the title, ironically, refers to an Idaho iron-on patch the narrator buys in Montana that he uses to convince others that he has actually visited the state (when, in reality, he turned around before getting there to avoid the cold). For the first third of the story, Hannah writes in almost diary form of runaway Confederate troops, his job at Missoula, his second and last wife Patty, his girl Anne, and his dog Jill, confessing self-reflexively to his readers his need to write: "As I write now, I still owe the IRS, and they've levied my salary and my writing money and they get all the money I get from this. And I am writing because I don't owe myself anything except writing" (*CM,* 19). Throughout "Idaho" and many of the other stories in *Captain Maximus,* Hannah discusses this practical need for writing as a way to pay the rent and fulfill personal obligations. Such interruptions in the narrative destroy the illusion of fiction and heighten the autobiographical nature of the story.

The story grows even more personal as it begins to focus upon Hugo and McGuane, for Hannah uses the two authors as a means of elaborating upon his personal philosophy of art and his repeated bouts with depression. In "Gunsmoke and Voodoo" Terrence Rafferty called "Idaho" "probably the plainest seven pages of fiction Hannah has ever published" (Rafferty, 677), and although Rafferty felt that this is the best story in the collection, he laments Hannah's use of prose to uncover what he believes is dishonest sentiment: "The voice *sounds* honest, personal, but the sentiment comes out all wrong—as it has to, conceived purely as material for use. What Hannah does with his own feelings is what he does with all the elements of his fiction, historical or imagined: he transforms them into private myths" (Rafferty, 677). In "Idaho" Hugo and McGuane both reach the stature of myth, not only because of the extent of their artistic ability, but also because of the friendship and kindness they exhibit toward Hannah. The narrator praises Hugo's "straight, clean, and full" poetry while thanking him for dispelling rumors that Hannah pulled a gun on writing students in Alabama; he admires McGuane for his ability to love his family, and he appreciates the praise McGuane lavishes upon his prose; and he even idolizes Jimi Hendrix and Stonewall Jackson, the musician for the truth in his lyrics and the general for his ability to overcome alcoholism.

But each of these myths serves a self-referential purpose for Hannah; all four men help to build the writer's ego and reassure him of the success of his craft. After Hugo's funeral, for example, the author returns to his room to listen to Hendrix and dream of Jackson, but his drunken thoughts turn to self-pity in spite of his efforts to move beyond them: "I was wild in my sorrow and my separation from my children. I was stepping away from that slobbering thug, self-pity. I thought I would try to" (*CM*, 22). Gaining strength from the music of Hendrix, the tales of Jackson, and his "friendships" with McGuane and Hugo, Hannah returns sober and happy to his children and his new woman, Margaret. Although his prize collection of guns are stolen by black men, Hannah finds satisfaction in the beauty of nature and his new lover. At the end of the story, Hannah writes, "I look down at my hand. It's not a gun. It's only a pencil. I am not going anywhere" (*CM*, 23), indicating in broken Hemingwayesque prose that his narrator has reached a level of acceptance foreign to him throughout much of his life. Unlike the protagonists in "Getting Ready," "Even Greenland," and "Fans," the narrator in "Idaho" is temporarily, at least, completely satisfied.

The ending of the story makes it clear that Hannah practices art for both public and private reasons. Like Hugo, McGuane, and Hendrix, Hannah wants his art to reach others, thereby making him "a giant in heart and body" (an expression he uses to describe McGuane), but he also needs writing to calm the violent, depressing, and even suicidal tendencies in himself. Unlike Hemingway, who shot himself in Idaho, Hannah uses his art to find the strength to overcome alcoholism and depression; for Hannah, art, as symbolized by the pen in the last sentence of the story, replaces the need for the pistol. His profession as a writer in "Idaho" literally saves him from the dark side of himself. Rather than resort to violence, like Harriman Monroe or Ray, the narrator realizes that through words he can accomplish more than he could with his pistol. The narrator in "Idaho" subordinates violence to art, a more potent and effective means of self-expression.

The structure of "I Am Shaking to Death," the story immediately following "Idaho" in the collection, illustrates tendencies of postcontemporary disjunctiveness, while the content remains sketchy and fragmented. The thin story line revolves around a narrator who is obsessed with a woman he spies at an illegal fat-farm near Yocona. The women who attend the camp are tied to ropes and dragged behind a jeep: "They agreed that they were ugly enough for things to happen to them and they would not be released until they were thin and better. And when they were thin, their attitudes had improved and they could leave or not, but you bet they were changed" (*CM*, 25). When he spies the same woman after church, much thinner now, in a black silk dress, the narrator pursues her with a vengeance. The rest of the story juxtaposes segments of their affair, from their sexual relationship to their trip to her home in Minneapolis, without providing details about how or why the relationship eventually dies.

As in "Idaho" the real focus of "I Am Shaking to Death" is the narrator who confesses, "I am trying to get better looking and wiser as I age. . . . Even trying to quit the cigarettes and the beer" (*CM*, 27). His love for the unnamed woman is never explained or elaborated; rather, he tells of a black man who stole his Cutlass automobile (not part of the same gang who absconded with his gun collection in "Idaho"), philosophizes about women and sexual needs, and emphasizes that the North is too cold for him. The title of the story may refer to the narrator and his once-obese girlfriend making love in the snow in Minneapolis, but it also implies a condition that the narrator finds himself in at the end of the short story—abandoned and alone: "I don't remember her house. Like me, she owed too much. I wish she'd read this and write me a letter" (*CM*, 29). "I Am Shaking to Death," when examined as a companion piece to "Idaho" in *Captain Maximus*, suggests almost a misuse of art for purely personal reasons. The narrator takes up the pen instead of the gun in "Idaho," but then uses it only to regain the woman who was physically his in "I Am Shaking to Death." The narrator temporarily overcomes alcoholism in "Idaho," but then literally experiences the shakes in "I Am Shaking to Death." In other words, the progress made by Hannah's persona in the first story seems to be negated by the second. If not read as companion pieces, the two stories seem too personal, sketchy, and internal; analyzed together, they chronicle the slow rise and steady fall of a writer struggling to find ways to use his art.

The sixth story in *Captain Maximus*, "It Spoke of Exactly the Things," also recounts a narrator's pursuit of a mysterious and unnamed woman, this time a mother he spies at Port of Call with her son, but, as in "I Am Shaking to Death," the focus of this disjunctive tale is not its almost nonexistent plot. "It Spoke of Exactly the Things" juxtaposes segments of prose bound together only by the opinions and prejudices of the narrator and his tendency to chase unapproachable women. The story begins with the narrator talking to his audience and himself in second person, encouraging himself to stumble drunkenly from Alabama to Abalone Cove, California; it proceeds by following the narrator's wanderings through San Pedro, Cabrillo Beach, Los Angeles, San Francisco, and, finally, back to Abalone Cove. Although the book is organized chronologically, Hannah uses a collage effect to bind together segments of prose detailing pieces of his pursuit and theories of existence. He is much more interested in tracing the narrator's thoughts about blacks, women, and California than in providing a traditional narrative with a strong central conflict.

But the narrator of "It Spoke of Exactly the Things" is much less satisfied and more destructive than the narrators of "Idaho" and "I Am Shaking to Death." Corrupted by several bad relationships, he speaks of women in demeaning and belittling terms such as "hag," "ghoul," and "hyena" (*CM,* 45). His philosophy of "eat or be eaten," and his hatred of the university where he works (he calls it a "neo-Grecian dump with a good ball team" where the "chairman fired back with drinking and eating female students"), drives him to San Pedro to watch windsurfing, listen to pilots talk, and watch ambulance drivers. The narrator is on the run from himself.

But even in California the narrator finds himself unable to escape from his self-hatred and disgust with mankind: "California is an excellent place for polishing your hatreds. The countryside is gorgeous and has made all the Californians into morons. They all deserve a drunken, abusive stepfather, like I was" (*CM,* 47). Unable to satisfy his needs with travel, he turns, like the narrator in "Idaho" and "I Am Shaking to Death," to a woman he spies coming out of Mary Star Church with her son who "had the complacent air of the petted one, the user, the incubated, the bloodsucker, the gigolo of his mother's blind affection" (*CM,* 48). Driven by loneliness, anger, and sexual desire, the narrator pursues the mother, attracted by her physical appearance and repulsed by her obvious wealth and collusive relationship with her son. As the narrator grows less happy with himself and his surroundings, his need for the woman grows more desperate. He begins to believe that only through her can he find hope for his future:

Beneath her breasts, in the slit of her blouse, was a curious thing—a tiny black tatooed butterfly.

This brought a sweat on me.
It spoke of exactly the things.
It gave hope. (*CM,* 49)

To avoid what he feels is the "absurb smallness" of himself and his "murky ratlike aggression," the narrator attacks the son by shooting whale shit at him with a sawed-off gun and eventually wins the woman for himself.

Like Laird in "Getting Ready" and John in "Even Greenland," achieving his goal provides only temporary satisfaction for the narrator. He brings his conquest back to the South where she plies him with drugs and drowns him in sex, making him believe momentarily that he has discovered something as "bold as love," but when the drugs run out the passion grows more carnivorous and the drinking begins again: "I banged the walls of space and time long enough. I don't have to lie. I think of the black butterfly and sometimes I can even remember her name" (*CM,* 53). Although the butterfly tattoo positioned between his lover's breasts initially promises salvation for the narrator—it, after all, "speaks of exactly the things" he desires and hopes to accomplish—its power soon dwindles, leaving the narrator with no sense of self-esteem and only faint, occasional memories. Hannah's narrators in *Captain Maximus* always look to external sources for fulfillment, when they should stop running or chasing long enough to examine the root of their prejudices and the real implications of their needs.

Even the disjunctive structure of the story suggests this need for self-searching. The story is organized around memory and association, not plot, conflict, or theme. A narrator who looks to material things and other people to achieve self-understanding contradicts what the structure of the story implies: that only through internal evaluation can the narrator learn more about himself. Sex, drinking, and travel represent false leads, paths that may speak of exactly the things the narrators need, but that ultimately dull the characters' senses to the internal struggles necessary to achieve real progress.

Nowhere is this more obvious in *Captain Maximus* than in the short story whose protagonist gives the collection its name: "Ride, Fly, Penetrate, Loiter." The four activities in the title symbolize not only the protagonist's, Ned Maximus's, fruitless pursuit of self-satisfaction, but they also represent the misguided focus of each of the narrators in the collection. The title reflects the circuitous pattern the narrators in Hannah's fiction experience whenever they attempt to initiate a quest for self-understanding: they begin by literally attempting to ride from their pasts; the ride, when unsuccessful, turns to flight; the flight is halted only by moments of "penetration," either sexual or spiritual; and when the temporary moments of penetration end, the loitering begins, only to be followed by the inevitable ride. The only comfort offered by such a pattern lies within the nonthreatening structure of the cycle itself—it may result in nothing, but it allows the possibility for temporary escape and freedom.

Narrated in almost diary form to the reader, "Ride, Fly, Penetrate, Loiter" is the most surfictional of the first seven stories in *Captain Maximus*. Hannah ignores linear narration, juxtaposes clumps of narrative related only by the protagonist, offers no direct meaning, and reflects on the authorial process. The focus of the story is the narrator, Ned Maximus (but called Maximum Ned), who flees Tuscaloosa and his teaching job at the university on a black-and-chrome Triumph motorcycle. The pettiness of the university town, from the "queers full of backbiting and rumors" to his wife who "was doing the standard frigid lockout at home," results in his becoming a drunkard, waiting impatiently for a friend to "attack the heart of the night" with him (*CM*, 36). Although he ironically explains that he does hold a position within such a society—"the drunkard lifts sobriety into a great public virtue in the smug and snakelike heart"—fulfilling such a position for the college community fills him with bad attitudes and self-hatred (*CM*, 36–37). He drives off to find the type of life Tuscaloosa could never offer.

The story traces achronologically the series of sketchy adventures Ned encounters on the road, all of them indistinguishable from similar tales of other narrators in *Captain Maximus*. He picks up a fake-Indian hitchhiker named Billy Seven Fingers who stabs him in the eye with Ned's own filet knife. Although the accident leaves him with a permanent eyepatch, it also gives Ned a gift resembling second sight that allows him to "see the heart of the night" (*CM*, 37). The dark eye under the patch, which "burns deep for language," inspires Ned to write about destiny and allows him to understand a variety of languages: white, African, Elizabethan, and Apache (*CM*, 38). The gift, however, does not improve the vision Ned has of the world as a place where "almost everybody sells used cars or dies early" (*CM*, 38); instead, he heads out into the real wasteland of America, not "that long, long, bloated epicene tract 'The Waste Land' by Eliot—the slide show of some smug librarian on the rag"; he deserts his students and "the standard shrill hag at the end of the bar," and runs from Dallas to the Louisiana town near where he grew up (*CM*, 40). Like other Hannah narrators, he finds the hope of salvation in a woman, Celeste, who he sees at a general store, and he has a vision that has left him changed ever since.

Ned sees in Celeste an unearthly beauty that makes each of the men in the town understand the paucity of their existence, inspiring them to reach conclusions alien to them before her arrival. One man recognizes suddenly that "life here is a belligerent sow, not a prayer," while another prays "for relief from this old charade, my mercantilia" (*CM,* 41). A customer yells, "We're naught but dying animals. Eve and then Jesus and us, clerks," while fighting with the owner who also reassesses his existence and profession: " 'Lost! Oh, lost!' the owner spoke. 'The redundant dirty clock of my tenure here!' " (*CM,* 42). Celeste stands unaffected as the owner, driven by lust for her and an unmanageable sense of self-deprecation, slays a dog with a shovel and "stomps at imagined miniature men on the floor" (*CM,* 42). This ambiguous vision, very possibly imposed onto the characters in the general store by Ned's overactive imagination, changes his life:

I have been sober ever since.
   I have just told a lie.
   At forty, I am at a certain peace. I have plenty of money and the love of a beautiful red-haired girl from Colorado. What's more, the closeness with my children has come back to a heavenly beauty, each child a hero better than yours. (*CM,* 40)

But the peace Ned reaches is as much of a lie as the sobriety he claims. The story ends with Ned threatening the reader: "You may see me with the eyepatch, though, in almost any city of the South, the Far West, or the Northwest. I am on the black and chrome Triumph, riding right into your face" (*CM,* 43). His relationship with the red-haired girl from Colorado and the ties with his family are only illusions—momentary stops in which he may loiter for a while, only to ride again in the future.

The unconventional structure in "Ride, Fly, Penetrate, Loiter" imitates the disheveled lives of Hannah's narrators. Relationships represent resting places, while truth lives only within the ability of Hannah's protagonists to experience illusions and record them in writing. Ned's eyepatch gives him no real supernatural power. It simply forces him to examine life with a renewed perspective, but the truth he sees is not reality; instead, the loss of his eye gives Ned the freedom to impose his reality upon those he sees, even the audience who reads what Ned records in print. The "certain peace" Ned ultimately reaches is undermined by his need to continue to gain new experience on the road, however false or illusionary that experience may be. Ned is doomed to ride into the faces of his audience, illustrating the fruitlessness of their existence and accusing them of joining the nonthinking, nonjudging public. Hannah may title the collection *Captain Maximus,* thus giving Ned superhero powers, but, ironically, Ned is less perceptive than the audience he accuses. He remains unable to change either himself or those around him; rather, he is only looking for another place to loiter, a temporary stay from the alienation of the road and the struggle with the self.

"Power and Light": Experiments with Montage

The final story in *Captain Maximus*, "Power and Light (An Idea for Film)," is a 40-page "script" written for Robert Altman to consider for the screen. Although the story was never filmed, it remains one of the more controversial, imagistic, and powerful pieces of fiction in Hannah's collection. Critics disagree about the worth of the story, but most admire its experimental structure and its visual strength. Doris Betts of *Book World* wrote that "Power and Light" should be "read the way energy pulsates, which comes with pleasures into the mind in the form of its title, as power and light,"[7] while George Stade of the *New York Times Book Review* felt that "cut by cut, the heart of a situation, a city even, is exposed. The scenes are visually sharp, but ambiguous in meaning, too complicated for summary."[8] James Wolcott called Hannah's vision in "Power and Light" a "punk ode," one that "has the daydreamy transitions of the films Altman made in the mid-Seventies, the dislocation of a mind floating free from its body on astral leave" (Wolcott, 33). Allen G. Shepherd III, in his article "The Latest Whiz-Bang: Barry Hannah's *Captain Maximus*," admired the piece's ambition, but felt that " 'Power and Light' reads like preparatory notes rather than finished fiction, or finished anything. Its inclusion in the volume and its engrossing four-tenths of it suggests, I should think, a shortage of material."[9] As Shepherd suggests, "Power and Light" reads more like preparatory notes than conventional prose, but it is this sense of unpolished writing that gives the story its visual strength and forces the reader to anticipate what lies ahead.

The seemingly clumsy style of "Power and Light" purposely imitates in prose the effect of montage upon the screen. Russian film director and theorist Sergei Eisenstein defined the principle of montage as an alternative to filming sequential scenes with a fixed camera. To prove that "absolute reality is by no means the correct form of perception,"[10] Eisenstein described each of his individual shots, not as elements of montage, but as montage *cells:* "A shot. A single piece of celluloid. A tiny rectangular frame in which there is, organized in some way, a piece of an event. 'Cemented together, these shots form montage' " (Eisenstein, 93). Filmic creativity and authorship, in other words, are reflected not by choice of subject, actor, or location, but by arranging and fusing disparate montage cells to produce a specific, emotional, intellectual, or descriptive effect. Until combined, shots are neutral pieces of recorded reality, but once juxtaposed in an original manner, neutrality dissolves into creativity. Montage, then, gave Eisenstein intellectual and psychological control over his material, allowing him to stimulate within the viewer emotion or thought without presenting detailed narrative.

Hannah seems especially influenced by Eisenstein's claim that "art is always conflict"; only through the collusion of independent shots can a director determine the dynamism, and thus the rhythm, of the film (Eisenstein, 45). Eisenstein believed that value begins with the worth of the shot, and art originates from the collision within individual montage "cells" and between combinations of two or more shots. By originating conflicts through the tension created by the struggle between synthesis and antithesis, a director creates art. In "Power and Light" Hannah originates 40 pages of montage cells, clumps of seemingly unrelated narrative bound together to create a new reality. Each clump of narrative has a visual strength of its own, and meaning is clarified only by understanding how each section is tied to the next. The success of "Power and Light" depends not only on its coherence as a piece of fiction, but, more importantly, on the strength of Hannah's visual associations. As a short story *or* as a script, "Power and Light" may read as a work-in-progress, but as "an idea for film" it successfully introduces a series of images that produce a powerful visual effect.

Although the many elements of Hannah's "script" are too complicated to recount in detail, several recurrent strains give the narrative a sense of unity and coherence. Hannah sets "Power and Light" in Seattle, and most of the characters he invents work for or use the power generated by the City Lights Powerhouse. Polly Buck, who lives with her lesbian roommate Larry Lynn Idol, works on the power lines, and Angel St. James is a dispatcher for the company. Both receive brown envelopes from a mysterious Eurasian who calls himself Sweed Truitt, warning them of an impending significant appointment. Maureen, a black woman who works as a crane pilot at the shipyard, also receives a brown envelope, as does Cornelia, a doctor who drinks more than she practices medicine. The story primarily revolves around these four women and the mysterious Eurasian who hides in a hotel room nearby with a stack of brown envelopes he sends periodically to each of them. Hannah uses the Eurasian and his mission to create the only tension in the story; as the women discuss the upcoming event foretold in the missives, he crosscuts between scenes of Sweed Truitt in his hotel room, watching and waiting for just the right moment to carry out his quest.

The men in each of the four women's lives are uniformly weak and dependent, especially when compared to the women who are their lovers, friends, and neighbors: Ruth has penned an X across the face of her ex-husband and now lives with Ian, an older man who watches too much television and takes no responsibility for Ruth's son Robbie; Maureen is constantly bothered by her junkie brother Lou, who begs her for money to support his heroin and cocaine addictions; Cornelia laments her husband's inadequate and barely functional sexual techniques; and Polly Buck, the central protagonist in "Power and Light," is happy to encourage her neighbors to believe that she too is a lesbian. Other men in "Power and Light" exhibit an inexplicable hostility toward the women they see daily. Polly's next-door neighbor Milton calls her a "twat on wheels" (*CM*, 71), and an unknown male power worker describes a female lineworker as a "cunt," much like the one he leaves at home (*CM*, 73). A second mysterious man with a white bulldog trails after the women to ask questions of the men who surround them, but he does not have the strength to approach them directly. Tension between the sexes, encouraged by the women's position of "power" in the city, runs throughout Hannah's script. Ironically, the mysterious letters pose some of the only real communication that exists between males and females. Although the letters frighten the recipients, they also promise something more, something to complement the satisfaction each experiences with her professional accomplishments.

Tying these characters together with other vignettes of life in Seattle are passages that describe the influence of the Seattle City Lights Powerhouse upon the entire city. The first image of the light pole, which Polly Buck will later climb during a thunderstorm, is of a workman in a hard hat who "twists back and forth at a connection" in an ominous manner (*CM*, 62). Hannah later reveals through what are probably the Eurasian's binoculars that this workman is not male: "Through a binocular's view: The workman twists, writhes. Just a minute. Some hair falls out. It's a woman" (*CM*, 63–64). From Ruth's perspective the audience later discovers that the line worker is dead:

At the T of the pole on the top of the building a tool is dropped. The body hangs limp, helmet tumbling down, long hair tumbling, waving in fog blasts.
Like dead.
The body shudders.
"It's a woman," says Ian.
"Yes. A Sister," says Ruth. (*CM*, 67)

This image of a woman sacrificed to the electrical needs of Seattle pervades "Power and Light." Hannah uses the vision as a constant reminder of the unnatural and life-threatening properties of electricity, and the all-encompassing influence it has over the lives in Seattle.

Constant authorial interruptions emphasizing the city's dependency on artificially made power and its more natural nemesis, water, tie the disparate elements of the story together. The line worker on the light pole dies because of a storm (a natural occurrence interrupting an unnatural one), and Hannah often describes the dangers Polly faces as she completes a day's work:

Fog rises as if the electricity is leaking out of the wires, and any fool knows that enormous electrical power and water like this don't mix without imminent death. We expect to see a frizzed, smoked girl shortly. . . .

This girl is chaining your breakfast together, citizen. She is hitching the light up for your asinine patio party, your old starlight teevee movies, your electric toothbrush, vibrator, Magic Fingers. (*CM,* 79)

In true montage fashion, Hannah interrupts a narrative section describing Ruth's lovemaking with Ian "with a first scan shot of City Lights Powerhouse" (*CM,* 90) to describe the origin of the electricity in her apartment: "Mister Kilowatt is dashing on his errands, to wires entering Ruth's splendid little hideaway apartment to wires coming out of her wall under her bed" (*CM,* 91). Although, as Paul Gray pointed out in his review of *Captain Maximus,* "Hannah's ordinarily vivid prose seems flattened towards objectivity" (*CM,* 70), in these passages he interrupts the narrative to include segments disapproving of Seattle's reliance upon electrical power.

Hannah's dependence on montage is also obvious in the arrangement of the story itself. By dividing the tale into short sections of narrative resembling the Tralfamadorean clumps of Kurt Vonnegut's *Slaughterhouse-Five,* Hannah juxtaposes conflicting images and crosscuts between the multitude of characters he introduces. For example, the story begins by describing a solitary jet's passage over the Cascades of Washington State with a chorus from Tchaikovsky providing the background music. The following segment, in Puget Sound, describes drunken fisherman discussing Indians and sex, and the third section presents a small blind boy named Little Willy who plays the harmonica on a Seattle street. Hannah often cuts from scenes of Polly Buck to those of the Eurasian in his hotel room and to those of the unknown man with the white bulldog inquiring about her, to provide the illusion of simultaneity. He even uses cinematic terminology to create transitions between one scene and the next: "Aeroscans of birds, all kinds of seabirds, sea, Puget Sound with boat life, wharfs, seals, howling noisy seabirds again, here and there a helicopter" (*CM*, 72). To move from the scene of Polly Buck fixing a broken power line, Hannah describes male figures who "come into focus," and to cut from the Eurasian on his way to eat at a restaurant, he writes, "Vision lowers on a huge lift crane at the shipyard" (*CM*, 85). Such authorial manipulation resembles that of a screenplay, in which the author details each of the camera shots and varying perspectives, but Hannah only uses this technique occasionally. He more often forces the reader to create transitions by juxtaposing two pieces of seemingly unrelated prose, tied together primarily by location and the mysterious brown envelope.

To further illuminate his own opinion of the characters and their relationships, Hannah also includes metaphorical passages, often describing animals or inanimate objects. After introducing, for example, Maureen's encounter with the white bulldog who does not like blacks, Hannah inserts a passage describing the solitude of the great walrus: "Behold the isolated walrus on a rock island! What is a walrus, what in hell is a walrus, anyway?" (*CM*, 77). The relationship he describes in the passage between a walrus and a sea cow comically parallels that between Maureen and Lou, and the ant farm Hannah inserts within the segment introducing Angel parallels her need to control her family: "Wait. There's something curious in the dining room. It's an ant farm, a whole civilization—queen, workers dithering in their tunnels" (*CM*, 69). Although often such shifts are confusing, these interruptions in narrative are carefully chosen and organized by Hannah. In "Power and Light" he builds layer upon layer of images, some figurative and others literal, to provide the machinations of an entire city, not just the relationships between its inhabitants.

The title of the story, "Power and Light," illustrates the complexity of the vision Hannah attempts to convey. On a literal level, the title obviously refers to the power and light derived from the City Lights Powerhouse in Seattle. On a more figurative level, the power signifies the strength of the female protagonists and their struggles to maintain equality in a society of males who are threatened by their accomplishments. Power also refers to the fight for dominance among creatures at all levels of life, from an ant farm to a city, and the need for companionship. The word "light" represents the product of the City Lights Powerhouse, as well as the paradoxical power of knowledge: the more the characters in the story are enlightened, the less they remain satisfied with their lives. The Eurasian, who derives power from his enigmatic position within the women's lives, also signals hope for their future—his brown envelopes indicate the promise as well as the threat of change.

The story ends with Polly Buck working diligently through a thunderstorm, although lightning strikes her helmet and even hits the white bulldog, who "flies off like a white small fat angel" (*CM,* 101). In the morning as Polly jumps down from the pole, the Eurasian meets her: "The brown-handed man in his leather jacket is there to catch her as she jumps down. She's repaired the electricity of Seattle and he's there to catch her. She looks at the man familiarly" (*CM,* 101). The story ends with Hannah's instructions about the final images on the screen:

> Ladies and Gentlemen,
> It's all power and light.
> Ruth comes to land in the beautiful F-14.
> The last frame is grainy, running with water.
> (*CM,* 101)

The conclusion holds promise for Polly, who recognizes the man who has been sending her letters; for Ruth, who lands her plane safely in spite of the storm; and for the city, whose final depiction is grainy with water, a source of natural, not artificial, power.

Hannah breaks new ground in "Power and Light," not only by writing about an area and subject alien to the South, but also by concentrating on four female characters. "Power and Light" shares with the other stories in *Captain Maximus* a thematic emphasis on the difficulty within relationships between the sexes, and a cynicism about Americans who find it impossible to balance material and spiritual needs, but he carries his experiments with narrative form further to imitate the cinema's reliance on the visual. In *Captain Maximus* Hannah continues to pull away from the traditional, chronological, bildungsroman structure he used in *Geronimo Rex* and *Nightwatchmen* toward a more metafictional tendency to break narrative into segments and rearrange them without regard to spatial and temporal conventions of fiction. Hannah's protagonists may still long to achieve "a certain peace," and, indeed, they may be closer to finding it, but his experiments with fragmented and disjunctive narrative form illustrate that their passage toward a satisfying resolution is growing increasingly difficult.

Chapter Five

Establishing the Community: The Juxtaposition of Images in *Hey Jack!* and *Boomerang*

In *Hey Jack!* (1987) and *Boomerang* (1989) Hannah both extends and modifies the montage techniques introduced in "Power and Light." He returns to the more familiar first-person narrative style, abandoning the objectivity and distance created within his "idea for film," yet because he retains the story's fragmented style and juxtaposed clumps of narrative, he is equally uninhibited by spatial and temporal restrictions. As in *Ray,* the narrators in *Hey Jack!* and *Boomerang* free the prose from the boundaries of chronology and place; in both novels, the single speaker delivers his stories from memory, association, and whim.

In the manner of oral tradition, the Korean who narrates *Hey Jack!* leads the reader through a series of stories involving recurring town characters, often shifting voice and persona to define the Mississippi town (resembling Hannah's own Oxford, Mississippi) as a microcosm of Southern society. In *Boomerang,* the most openly autobiographical of Hannah's fiction, Hannah himself serves as the narrator, carrying readers back and forth to moments in his life from his childhood through his third marriage and present teaching position.

The plot of neither novel is new: Hannah still explores (and exploits) the random violence and desperate acts of a group of Southerners whose knowledge of life is paradoxically both restricted and enlightened by the boundaries of heritage and family. But in both works Hannah continues to experiment with structure and organization: he distorts conventional space and time, imitating the formlessness of storytelling and the immediacy of cinematic image, in order to establish a personal and sometimes sentimental vision of the sense of community that justifies the two narrators' affection for the South.

Hey Jack! Imitating the Oral Tradition

The Korean narrator of *Hey Jack!,* finally identified as Homer only on the last page of the novel, writes in a disjointed journal form to distinguish his life and to share the tales of his Mississippi home before time destroys memories of his past. To describe his perceptions, he admittedly shifts personas throughout the novel: "You will find me changing voices as I slip into the—let us say—*mode* of the closer participant."[1] Hannah uses these shifts to carry readers from one sequence to the next without transition or explanation. To describe the various perspectives of others who live in the Mississippi town and to preserve the sense of oral tradition, Hannah moves occasionally from first- to third-person, presenting incidents without indicating passage of time or change in location. Only the age of the participants and their relationship with other members of their family indicate specific time, while location depends entirely on the context of a tale, not on a logical or organized movement. The choppy vignettes vary in length from one to ten pages, separated from other segments by the typographical emblem of a small smiling sun. The vignettes in *Hey Jack!* are more highly developed and clearly defined than those in "Power and Light." They describe in more detail the backgrounds of a variety of characters from the rural South: the coke-snorting rock star Ronnie Foot, the hypochondriachal professor, the psychologically disturbed dentist, the war-torn Wally Cooper, and the enigmatic Jack, a character whose recurring stories and charisma help to tie the disparate fragments of the novel together.

Although critics admired Hannah's verbal ingenuity and mastery of Southern voices in *Hey Jack!,* many objected to the fragmentary narrative and rambling organization of the novel. Albert E. Wilhelm of *Library Journal* complained that Hannah's "story is disappointingly sparse. He provides intriguing characters and antecdotes but little sustained narrative,"[2] while Michiko Kakutani of the *New York Times* criticized Hannah's inability to sympathize with his characters: "There is little affection, generosity or understanding in Homer's—or for that matter—Mr. Hannah's depiction of these people; and as a result they seem a random collection of misfits whose eccentricity, selfishness, and stupidity mean nothing."[3] Thomas R. Edwards of the *New York Times Book Review* wrote that "geography, local culture, and a sense of his precursors—especially Faulkner—seem to be interfering with his performance,"[4] and Jim Kobak in *Kirkus Review* asked, "How long can Hannah hide behind his obnoxious 'personae' "?[5] It is true that in his experiments with style and structure to create a multitude of voices resembling the sound and history of an entire community, *Hey Jack!* pays homage to Faulkner novels such as *As I Lay Dying* and *The Mansion*. But unlike Faulkner, Hannah shows little interest in creating either a sustained narrative or a mythic persona; rather, he focuses more upon the voice of the community than that of any individual within it. Richard Eder recognized this emphasis in his review of *Hey Jack!* in the *Los Angeles Times:* "Homer's wandering cogitations, his tales, his pleasures and his anguish all ramble to a purpose. They test and reveal the tensile struggle of a cord that is never really loosed; that binds him to his deadly memories, that binds his Southern community and perhaps all communities to their own."[6] Hannah purposely imitates a random collection of cinematic shots in *Hey Jack!,* fused together not to sustain a conventional narrative, but to give the reader brief vignettes that describe the life and character of a small Mississippi town.

To provide exposition and define character in "Power and Light" Hannah links protagonists to characteristic visual motifs. Polly Buck is recognizable because of the hardhat that she often wears, representing both her independence and her ability to survive in a male-dominated profession, while Maureen is similarly defined by the crane she operates and the plane she pilots. The mysterious man on the street is always identifiable by his white bulldog, the Eurasian by his brown envelopes, Cornelia by her alcohol, and Ian by his television set. In *Hey Jack!* Hannah softens this objective, impersonal method of character reference, while still relying on techniques that resemble those used in the cinema. Homer tells stories to his acknowledged audience, each within a vignette or expanded over a series of noncontinuous vignettes, and the incidents and details of these tales become motifs to define individual characters. The hypochondriachal professor, for example, is identified not by any single item, but by his fear of life, his selected protégés, and the accident that ends his life: "When he was taking a leak behind his car, his own car . . . it rolled backwards on his greatly steep drive, wildly in neutral, and rose over him, knocking his head to the pavement. Thereupon his head exploded in horrible pale matter" (*HJ,* 5). Such tall tales, delivered with respectful solemnity by Homer to his audience, give his subjects life and make them memorable throughout the novel. Hannah often avoids naming these characters; instead, he labels them either by profession or by incident, imitating a small town's tendency to exaggerate the characteristics of its inhabitants through generations of storytelling.

In addition to this use of vignettes two distinct plot lines bind the story and its characters together. The first traces Homer's efforts to come to terms with the violence he experienced in Korea and to become part of the community for which he holds great affection. The second recounts Jack's violent struggle to protect his daughter Alice from her destructive relationship with hometown rock star Ronnie Foot. Although Hannah weaves both plots together by juxtaposing Homer's vignettes with his conversation with Jack, he concentrates in *Hey Jack!* upon Homer's life and his opinion of his fellow townspeople. Now 56-years-old, white-haired, handsome, and horny, Homer is a creature of habits. He drinks only rye (four drinks a day every day), and smokes Luckies (rarely more than the 15 per day he allots himself). He is in love with a 41-year-old woman, who once dated the town's dentist, now dead from a heart attack. When he finally marries her, Homer is the conventional picture of success. He and his wife rent a mansion built in 1870 (with two magnolias in the front yard), drive a Porsche, play with their dogs and cats, and mow their 120-acre lawn. Homer is happy with his wife and his marriage: "She went around half naked in shorts and a bound-up tee shirt. It was certainly nice to be married, having all the nooky and the smiles" (*HJ*, 97). Although he sometimes argues with his wife, the primary conflict in Homer's life is the past's continual influence upon the present. Not unlike Bobby Smith in *The Tennis Handsome,* Homer finds himself haunted by his experiences during the war in Korea and parallel experiences in his beloved Mississippi town.

Almost everything in his hometown triggers memories of his inadvertent heroism, from a war movie he sees on television to his concern over poverty-stricken blacks who make a hero out of pop singers such as Michael Jackson. Even aged blues singer Hooray Bugger reminds Homer of the possibility of death, encouraging his memory to replay his most momentous war battle: "Ignorance ran like a wind, smelling of garlic and hot machine-gun bullets. The ejected smell of howitzers went off and made the snow give way. All of the squad had gathered into the black circle, rubbing against the warm shells, ducking and rubbing. Until I got sick of it and said charge. Surprised the Chinese. Surprised myself. I was firing two carbines, one in each hand. Then I fell down when I was hit in the knee. But I'd frightened away their whole line" (*HJ*, 120). Although Homer confesses that a smell reminding him of Choisin caused him to go nuts for a month, he shares neither Bobby Smith's guilt over his role in the war nor his inability to live in the present because of past slaughters. Homer is obsessed with the Korean conflict, so much so that he reads a book about the Eighth Army in Korea while at a friend's wake, but he is ultimately reassured by the stories he tells and by the survivors of natural and emotional catastrophe: "I live to say this. Jack lives" (*HJ*, 131). Combining the need to survive with the desire to achieve personal gratification, all within a humanist framework, is a challenge that Homer attempts to meet throughout *Hey Jack!*. Unlike other

Hannah protagonists, Homer balances personal needs with humanistic concerns; he helps others, but not to the exclusion of his own desires.

His fragmented achronological stories serve a dual purpose: they describe the town and its inhabitants to the readers and they teach Homer lessons in moderation and behavior. The dentist, for example, who was once his wife's lover, is unable to overcome one rash deed performed by three black men who worked for him. Although he overpaid the workers, giving them free service at the emergency room and buying them cigarettes and food, they betrayed him by quitting and leaving the gates of his hogpen open, resulting in most of the animals' deaths: "He could not reconcile himself with such spite" (*HJ*, 9). He seeks counseling from a psychiatrist in Meridian, and when he is threatened with the truth about his potential homosexuality, he flees. At 66, deserted by his wife and his sons, the dentist remains an eccentric loner with "an amiable long-haired cur with the great warm brown eyes of his wife" (*HJ*, 15). When the son of one of his ex-workers shows up at the farm expressly to confuse and "mess with" him, the dentist dies on the spot of a heart attack: "And this is how our dentist friend went away, already dead but leaving a handsome lean, gray-haired corpse behind" (*HJ*, 18). The dentist, like the professor, brings about his own demise by refusing to understand or delve into the "self." He never returns to the psychiatrist who attempts to make him face the truth. Stories such as these teach Homer to accept his role as a soldier in Korea, for only through such acceptance can he avoid more senseless behavior.

Hannah's use of brief, oddly juxtaposed vignettes reflects the ebb and flow of Homer's thoughts. For example, after recounting a conversation with Jack, Homer tells us briefly of his hatred for Harmon, a tall and handsome high school graduate who "is a large chickenshit who likes to beat women" (*HJ*, 24). Homer detests Harmon's cocky assuredness, blind prejudice, and unjustified conceit: "He thinks he is a free power. He doesn't have the guts to enlist in the service. He'd rather stay around town and burn gasoline, being a delivery boy at a grease palace" (*HJ*, 23). Eventually, however, Homer reveals the real reason he feels "that people like young Harmon would better serve each other by going back up in the hills and committing incest man on man"; Harmon reminds Homer of the sorry soldiers in Korea who "couldn't wait to get back home where the *real* wreckage was" (*HJ*, 24). Harmon has a place in *Hey Jack!* because he occupies a space in Homer's mind: he represents the destructive impulses that thrive within the town Homer loves. Through Harmon's story, Homer learns the dangers of conceit and prejudice, and he also recognizes that dependence upon a small town can inhibit as well as encourage personal growth.

Another destructive force, this time in the character of Wally Cooper, Marine veteran of Korea, parallels Homer's own situation in the town. Homer recognizes in Cooper's advertisement for "a wife who will be a confidante and friend" the same pride and horror he feels each time he remembers Chinese field armies crossing the Yalu in October 1950. Because Cooper, a Korean veteran with a nervous disorder, never receives a reply to his advertisement, he begins to resent those who have become the successful artists he wanted to be. He makes death threats over the phone to students and professors who have private art showings. Intrigued by Cooper's situation and his particular brand of lunacy, Homer pursues the story, discovering that the Marine vet was shot three times at Pusan: "That's all I needed to know. He wasn't just a nut. . . . I found a kind of mirth and even necessity in Wally Cooper's death threats. Had he called me I'd have been flattered" (*HJ*, 49–50). In Homer's opinion, the worth of each individual in the several vignettes of *Hey Jack!* is directly related to his or her contributions to the community. According to Homer, Harmon deserves to die because his self-interest actually destroys society; Cooper deserves to live because his death threats hurt no one in the community and reflect an inner need for peace and acceptance.

Other vignettes describe eccentric characters in less detail than those of the doctor, dentist, and Cooper, but each occupies a particular place in Homer's thoughts. The dentist's son is possessed with the amount of junk Americans throw away daily, and be begins to hide objects he finds: "I drive around and see all the wonderful junk lying out there. I want all of it. What this country has left behind is three whole other countries" (*HJ*, 39). Obsessed with what he believes is the real junk—TV, newspapers, religion, even his wife's conversation—he leaves society to find a place where he can make sense of the world and its "connections." The doctor's daughter Delia is equally confused. After a brief affair with the town's local rock hero, she becomes addicted to cocaine, and then Ritalin. She wanders around aimlessly, avoiding the bill collectors at the house, "trying not to remember how [she] drank from the water left in the commode" (*HJ*, 116). Both the doctor and the dentist affect more than just themselves; they leave behind a legacy of pain and suffering that their children cannot overcome. Through their tales Homer realizes that each action sets off a series of chain reactions, and that members of a community are responsible for considering how their actions will affect others.

Many of these stories resemble tales passed around on porches or in the old town square. Although Homer admits early in *Hey Jack!* that these storytellers have not been flatteringly portrayed in other novels, he stresses that "you cannot ignore their wisdom and you cannot ignore the fact that it takes a certain strength to sit out in such a hot shade in the summers and watch the cars and young scoundrels" (*HJ*, 2). But Homer weaves each of his tales in the oral tradition of the men who reflect in rocking chairs for a specific purpose: to illustrate the tapestry of joy and despair that occurs in his town, and within each one of its inhabitants, every day. Even though Homer narrates most of the tales in *Hey Jack!*, because Hannah fuses his stories together without transition he creates a multitude of voices from the town, all raised simultaneously to provide a picture of the history and tradition of a Southern community.

But it is the second plot line, tracing the history of Jack and his family, that parallels Homer's own situation in Korea and leads him to uncover the destructive impulses that destroy the fragile unity created by place and time. Like the vignettes of the professor, the dentist, and the Marine veteran, Jack's tales are fragmentary and achronological, but unlike Homer's other Mississippi stories, Jack's life runs continuously throughout *Hey Jack!*, making his character almost as complete as the narrator's.

Once a sheriff in Lexington, Kentucky, Jack Lipsey resigned when two thugs stabbed him and stole the trophy he won in 1953: "He'd had it with being a sheriff. With awards. With everything that made you noticeable, everything that made you the dumb bull's eye" (*HJ*, 62). He married a Kentucky aristocrat who shot herself while in a South Carolina mental institution, and moved to Mississippi "so that he could build himself into a strong man again, piece by piece, no thugs jumping on him, just mosquitos and his old age" (*HJ*, 62). Homer admires the 76-year-old Jack for his moderation and good sense, but at the beginning of the novel he does not know or understand the storekeeper. Although Homer tells his audience that Jack "has never been an urgent historian of his own past," that "Jack is no gabby philosophizer," he encourages Jack to tell him of his three previous marriages, his two daughters, and his career teaching criminal science at a small college in Maryland (*HJ*, 20). Unlike the other vignettes in *Hey Jack!*, however, Jack's is not a story defined by facts, history, or detail; instead, as the novel progresses, Homer begins to understand that Jack's life has been a complex series of flirtations with violence, and that he faces a final crisis that will determine the quality of Jack's remaining years.

In his youthful choice of professions, Jack encountered violence both theoretically and physically. As a teacher, he instructed others in the machinations of the criminal system, and as a sheriff, he punished those who broke the law. Homer, however, admires Jack's ability to balance aspects of his life, from drinking to smoking, and he views Jack as a figure who breaks with southern stereotypes: "He has been a man of action, and now he is quite at peace as a shopkeeper, always polite but never groveling, as you find in the false little country restaurants hereabouts. ('Hi, y'all! Come back, honey!') Christ the South has been pickled in the juice of its own image" (*HJ,* 20). As Homer grows closer to Jack in the course of the book, sharing his Luckies and rye and even playing golf with the storekeeper, he discovers that only one man could bring Jack to violence, rock star Ronnie Foot.

Son of a poor, white, redneck family, Foot grew up with an ill great-grandfather restrained to his bed, a grandfather addicted to codeine and frightened of blacks, and a mother and father whose only profession was, according to Homer, "being dumb and nuts" (*HJ,* 4). Much like Faulkner's Snopes family, but without their cunning and guile, the Foots live uncomfortably with their wealth, dying slowly in the rotting mansion Ronnie has built for them: "It was built fast and is already turning into doo doo, things falling out of the ceiling, black widows and brown recluses having a field day all over the corner. At night the roaches come in and heave off huge crumbs, which are everywhere" (*HJ,* 33). While Gramps gets drunk on vodka and shoots at chickens from a second-floor window, Double Gramps is in a coma and Mama and Daddy fix taters and watch television. Ronnie's money has taken away what little sense of purpose the Foots ever had. Hannah himself describes them as the thinnest, most stereotypical characters in the novel.

Foot has returned to his hometown, Jack feels, primarily to wield his superficial power as a rock star upon unsuspecting women who find his good looks and shallow worldliness appealing: "You fight for freedom in Korea. And myself at Normandy. Later with Patton. This is not freedom. He's come back to the county. Everything that America can buy was not good enough for him. He's come back to destroy his own people, and the best of them. A rooster, a chickenshit Sherman, turned back on his own" (*HJ,* 30). Jack's hatred of Ronnie Foot is accentuated by the 33-year-old rock star's affair with his youngest daughter, the 40-year-old Alice. Calling upon all of his experience, Jack cannot understand her attraction for Foot, and tries throughout the novel to prevent what he sees as her inevitable path toward suicide (like her mother before her). He interrupts her sexual unions with Foot, drives golf balls into the window of the Foot mansion, and even inadvertently inspires Homer to borrow a .38 and shoot at the house. But neither Homer nor Jack is able to prevent the inevitable: "Alice is going to die and the date lies almost delicious in my mind, as if I'd bitten off a piece of the calendar" (*HJ,* 86).

As Jack becomes increasingly obsessed with his daughter's relationship with Foot, Homer finds himself becoming involved. He uncovers the history of Foot's destructive relationship with the professor's daughter Delia, and even confronts Alice directly about her father's concern, leading to a brief but passionate affair between the Korean and Jack's daughter.

Homer's growing concern for Alice not only initiates an argument between Jack and his wife, but it also brings back memories of the violence in Korea. In spite of Jack's pleading and Homer's interference, Alice quits her job and becomes addicted to cocaine and Ronnie. She travels with him, subordinating her life-style to his, and is eventually killed by the millionaire rock star: "I have tried to delay the news. I have tried. Foot got in a bad mood and killed her with Gramps' .22" (*HJ*, 127). When Alice tries to console Ronnie after his great-grandfather dies, he places a coke bottle on her head and tries to shoot it off, but he misses and kills Alice, a murder he describes at the trial more "as capital boredom than capital crime" (*HJ*, 131).

Alice's death fuses in Homer the violence he experiences in Korea with that in his hometown. At Alice's wake, he reads a historical account of the Eighth Army's strategy against the Chinese and MacArthur's justification for attack, and he associates her death with those in Korea:

Oh, Alice. Hubba hubba, girl. After making it back from the Chinese and with my silver star all dogged away behind me, after having that night of you, and then yourself, a ghost talking to me, and then the last phone call, and then you dead.
    Killed by a simple stupid millionaire rock star.
    I was pulling my trigger finger in the air again. (*HJ*, 131)

Although Homer sees Jack as a man of peace, the relationship between Alice and Ronnie proves that such a judgment is biased and untrue. Both Jack and Homer have the same tendencies toward violence that are exhibited within other vignettes in *Hey Jack!*. As Richard Eder writes in "A War Memorial in the Mind," "The infection of war is as real as if real killing had taken place" (Eder, 12). Peace is impossible for either Jack or Homer as long as the Ronnie Foots of the world infest communities and place the immediate needs of the self before the needs of the town. Alice's death is ultimately as inevitable as the murders that occur at the Choisin Reservoir—both episodes of violence reflect a nihilistic universe whose inhabitants seek meaning through relationships with others. And that is ultimately the driving force behind Homer's narrative: to discover a purpose and logic to a world that denies him meaning. *Hey Jack!* is the Korean's effort to make sense of history and his place within it.

Splitting the narrative into sections resembling cinematic montage, each imitating Homer's memory and struggle to make sense of past and present events, reflects the thematic fragmentation. The stories of the town and its inhabitants are fused within the narrator's mind, much like juxtaposed shots within a film, and Hannah's emphasis on the visual quality of the narrative indicates the significance Homer places on each of the townspeople's tales. He often ties together unrelated narratives to illustrate the random nature of memory. For example, Homer philosophizes about the violence hidden within the hearts of Southern communities: "The Civil War was not started by Harriet Beecher Stowe, as Lincoln said, or by Sir Walter Scott, as Mark Twain said, or by economics, as somebody said. It was started by a thousand towns like this, bored out of their minds" (*HJ*, 64). He also warns readers not to get close to him: "Nothing is sacred, I tell everything" (*HJ*, 64). Immediately following this statement, he describes with admiration a coyote he and Jack spied on a country trip, and the next segment describes his wife's grandfather and a family gathering at Neshoba County. None of the vignettes builds upon one another conventionally. Homer neither indicates the time of each segment, nor does he attempt to suggest a causal relationship between his opinion of the South, his description of coyotes, or his memories of his wife's grandfather. Instead, he strings together the images as he remembers them, forcing the audience to form its own associations.

Such a fragmented structure contributes to the reality of the vision Hannah attempts to convey to his readers. In an interview with Jan Gretland, Hannah explained that although he loves Faulkner's description of the South, he does not find it realistic: "If you're cynical and arrogant, you might begin looking at the South as just existing for movies. That's how I think of Faulkner—I mean, he invented a beautiful cast; Yoknapatawpha is movie-Oxford. It is imagination land. I don't think it does any good for these Japanese people to come here and get on a bus and go out in the sticks to look for Eula Varner and the Snopeses. They're not there. They never really were" (Gretland, 233). Hannah's "cast of the imagination" is based upon his personal recognition of reality within Southern communities. Although *Hey Jack!* is narrated by a Korean character, Hannah ultimately is writing about himself and the people with whom he has shared his life. Like Faulkner, he concentrates upon the violence hidden beneath the surface of the South, but he more obviously continues to reuse and reinterpret autobiographical information. Juxtaposing vignettes in cinematic form gives Hannah the freedom to explore the multitude of voices existing within the minds of each of his narrators—from Harriman Monroe to Homer—and to experiment with the methods by which his narrators retain and associate memories. Hannah breaks from conventional narrative in *Hey Jack!* in order to record a realistic South that struggles both to sever and honor its past.

Boomerang: Stretching the Boundaries of Fiction

In *Boomerang* Hannah abandons the thinly disguised autobiographical narrator of *Hey Jack!* to write more openly about the family, friends, and conflicts that have influenced his life and career. The book jacket advertises *Boomerang* as Hannah's "own tender weaving of novel and autobiography,"[7] but as Sybil Steinberg wrote in her review of the novel for *Publishers Weekly,* "When one encounters descriptions of 'the great publisher Sam Lawrence' arriving in a stretch limousine or mention of 'the horrible brilliant Gordon Lish,' one cannot help but speculate over the decision to call this fiction."[8] Although *Boomerang* contains the disclaimer that "this novel is a work of fiction. Names, characters, places, and incidents either are the product of the author's imagination or used fictitiously," the autobiographical elements of *Boomerang* are obvious. Using a fictional framework, Hannah adapts recognizable incidents from his own life, such as his five days in a mental institution, his first two unsuccessful marriages, his admiration for Willie Morris, and his friendship with the McGuanes (about whom he also writes in *Captain Maximus*).

Using the symbol of a boomerang to represent the movement of memory and the influence of the past upon the present, Hannah describes recognizable incidents from his own life in order to provide an honest depiction of the South. His "fictional" narrator is named Barry, adding to the autobiographical bias of the novel. In *Boomerang* Hannah leaps from one memory to the next, sharing the failures of Barry's earlier marriages, his strained relationships with his children, and his friendships with other writers and actors. The honesty with which he recounts incidents that resemble those of his own life is both satisfying and unsettling: *Boomerang* reads almost like a diary in which Hannah bares the intricacies and complexities of his personal life using an experimental, loosely fictional structure.

In spite of Steinberg's concern about the autobiographical nature of Hannah's fiction, she praises the "sweeps of narrative that are soaringly, daringly, brilliantly original" and "the intelligence and visceral emotions Hannah rams onto a page"; her primary criticism is that the book "staggers under a load of extraordinary writing which seems somehow lazily shovelled together" (Steinberg, 57). Joanna Kennedy, in her review of *Boomerang* for the *New York Times Book Review,* wrote that "no new ground is broken in

Boomerang; what we get from Mr. Hannah is instinct and impact over plot, as always."[9] But she too praised Hannah's "clear, spare prose" and his "distinctive raconteur's voice that could only be Southern" (Kennedy, 23).

Like other postcontemporary writers, Hannah breaks the fragmented narrative of *Boomerang* by adding self-reflexive passages that discuss his narrator's writing and his need to fictionalize his life. For example, in the chapter "2000" Hannah interrupts his discussion of publisher Sam Lawrence and the Civil War to emphasize the independence and strength writing has given him: "I've personally been beaten so many times that death looks like a pussy to me. Come on, little dude, show me something. I've spoken my head off in nine books and have twenty lovers and friends" (*B*, 138). In the chapter "Thinking" he humorously reminds readers that although they are reading a text, the author is always behind the narrative: "Women exchangable like shells coming back and thrown off in the weeds from a howitzer landguarded by three poor fuckers from Germany or the U.S.A. or does it matter—the exchangable women like thrown-out vessels wherein used to place some cock, etc.—where the shit is the end of this sentence, Faulkner?" (*B*, 100). For the first time, Hannah even has characters address his narrator by his own first name, and he openly discusses Barry's relationships with the writers Norman Mailer, Alex Haley, Hunter Thompson, and Jim Harrison, and relatives including his grandmother, children, and uncles. The tone of the novel is confessional, but Hannah manages to achieve some distance between reader and writer by inventing a structure that fragments reality into blocks of seemingly unrelated narrative memories, much like editing within a film.

Although Hannah divides *Boomerang* into 15 chapters, he uses a structure very similar to that in *Hey Jack!*. As Joanna Kennedy points out, "Random vivid episodes are held together by three boomerang throwing sessions, which give a remarkably complete impression of his nearly 50 years" (Kennedy, 23). Form defines and reflects characterization in *Boomerang,* especially that of the narrator, whose thoughts control the flow of the narrative while his hands control the throw of the boomerang. Like Homer in *Hey Jack!*, the narrator of *Boomerang* juxtaposes images based on memory and associations in a sparse, cinematic form. An image of a harpist who played with Hannah in the Jackson Symphony Orchestra will trigger the memory of a harpist he encounters 20 years later in Venice, California; the story of Art Krebs, a retired army major, brings to mind Barry's friend Quisenberry, a commander in the the Navy Reserve Air Force; and the memory of Quisenberry reminds Barry of Hoyt Weems, the disgruntled high school football coach, "a raw, tough, ugly soldier, who wanted to talk about people burning up alive in tanks" (*B*, 24). *Boomerang* is more roughly chronological than *Hey Jack!*, but Hannah does not bind his autobiographical novel to either place or time. The first chapter, "Tiny," recounts Hannah's youthful battles with his childhood friends and introduces the central image of the boomerang (ordered from the back of a comic book for $1.98), but in following chapters, as the boomerang triggers within Hannah a variety of memories, he achronologically strings together images from his life.

For example, in the second chapter, "Oxford," Hannah describes a tall black man walking with a cane and gathering cans (possibly for recycling); a Kentucky man who killed his girlfriend; his narrator's own guitar-playing son, second marriage, and life as a bachelor; a man who works at the animal shelter; and an 84-year-old woman who never leaves her kitchen. The effect he achieves resembles an Altman film (for whom Hannah wrote "Power and Light"), and Hannah even pays homage to the "kind and brilliant" Altman when he writes about Barry's experiences as a screenwriter in California. In eight pages Hannah juxtaposes five images that for him define Oxford. Each image is separated only by the two typographical figures of transparent blocks (resembling the figure of the smiling sun that breaks the narrative in *Hey Jack!*). Like Altman's *Nashville* and *A Wedding*, the chapters present a number of perspectives indicating various opinions of life in Oxford. Although Hannah ties *Boomerang* together using Barry's narrative perspective, by juxtaposing without transition a variety of stories, he creates a multitude of voices, each raised to express its own vision of the communities in Mississippi.

The central voice in *Boomerang* is still Hannah, however, and like the narrators from other Hannah novels such as *Ray* and *Hey Jack!*, the protagonist of his most recent novel is of dubious morality. In the chapter "Lost Pilots" Hannah confesses to readers that his narrator is indeed "a terrible man": "In fact, I move through life without a conscience" (*B*, 42). Hannah uses this lack of a conscience to explain Barry's insensitivity to women and to defend his chauvinistic attitude toward his wives. He seems to understand and even dislike his misogynistic treatment of women, but he rarely acts to alter his views. In *Boomerang*, for example, Barry suggests that only sexual activity will save the women he knows: "I must rescue our women. There's only one way to do it, ladies: make a big pot roast . . . and then get naked except for your high-heeled shoes, if you've got any legs and fanny left. He'll eat the roast and then sleep, dreaming about some bitch five counties away. You've done everything to please him but it's not enough. Good thing I finally get up and take care of the little women, heh

heh" (*B*, 45). Like his friend Yelverston, Barry claims that "most women want a glass of white wine on the rocks and a hard member underwater . . . and a hundred thousand to shop with" (*B*, 125), and he makes it clear throughout *Boomerang* that he is capable of offering women all that they need (except the money). Even the comparisons he affects supposedly to analyze and understand women are demeaning: "It goes without saying that a woman with good legs in sandals beats the hell out of a greasy breakfast with grits and comments about money" (*B*, 128). Remarks such as these make it clear that Hannah intends to portray his narrator as largely responsible for the failure of his earlier marriages, and Barry's constant dreams of infidelity illustrate that his third marriage is tenuous at best. In fact, he admits that whenever his wife and he "live together in the gray house hating each other," he abandons her: "She falls asleep and I try to slip out and get next to strange nooky but she always wakes up and tracks me down in her gown and bedroom slippers" (*B*, 122). Throughout *Boomerang* women are depicted as harpies and monsters, and although the narrator attempts to portray his most recent marriage honestly, he does not provide enough information for the reader to make informed judgments about any of the supporting characters.

In fact, determining motives in *Boomerang* for characters such as Barry's two ex-wives is extremely difficult, primarily because Hannah focuses the novel almost exclusively around the memory of his admittedly "terrible" protagonist. Many of the other characters in *Boomerang* are defined only by how they directly affect the narrator, or how they contribute to his string of memories. To describe his first wife, for example, Barry lists the problems she had living with him, providing only sketchy facts about *her* life and past:

My first wife worked hard for me and rushed me into marriage. She was an army brat who thought my parents were rich. She was a painter and a lover and a wife, but foremost she made sure we were married. She hated all my friends. She had the great talent for taking the heat out of any situation that gave me joy. She had no friends. Everything scared her.

But now she is better. (*B*, 32–33)

Barry's second wife and marriage are dismissed just as casually as his first, and although he admits that he "could not bear the legacy of physicians and wives who never taught their kids any guts or sense," be blames her for the inevitable divorce: "My second wife was a beautiful book-burner from Nebraska. She had enough of me and threw me out" (*B*, 67). As in an autobiography, cause and motive are subordinated to a presentation of the facts (from Barry's narrow and egocentric perspective). Hannah rarely provides detailed reasons for the failures of his first two marriages; instead, he offers only his versions of the facts behind his protagonist's life and leaves them for the reader to interpret.

Hannah does describe Barry's third marriage to Susan, to whom Hannah dedicates the novel, in more detail than his earlier relationships, but his ambivalence about the future of the venture is made apparent by means of his contradictory views of their relationship. On the one hand, Barry praises his third wife, calling her "my sweet faithful wife Susan" (*B*, 63), and he describes life with her as bountiful: "It is like the Garden of Eden with a woman who is so good-looking I took a Polaroid picture of her lying in bed in Biloxi with her breasts showing" (*B*, 95). He even offers advice to his readers about how to stay married, based on what he has learned in his struggles with Susan: "Take time to write everybody a love note that you love. Take time to examine your wife's anatomy and her clean clothes for you and take care of your children" (*B*, 146). But, on the other hand, in spite of the praise Barry sometimes offers Susan, he despises her ability to make him face himself: "I hate her often. She challenges the thing: the *thing*. The thing itself" (*B*, 95). The "thing," for Barry, could be any number of aspects of his life: his own inability to commit to relationships; the unreasonable demands he makes of his partners; his tendency to seek out temporary sexual liaisons; even his penchant for self-adulation. Hannah elaborates further about his narrator's problem with his most recent marriage when he first introduces Susan to the reader: "Another Sunday, 1988. All this day I've worried about what to do with this third marriage. It is a cold day in April and my wife has never offered to lick me or serve me food" (*B*, 41). He resents Susan's feminist viewpoints, which circumvent the sexual favors that Barry feels he deserves because of his time spent in Vietnam, but proudly announces that he has curbed her feminist viewpoints with his "masculinity": "She's off the picket line now. My great sullen manliness is controlling her and she has no self-esteem anymore, which is exactly the way I want it" (*B*, 42).

Hannah's narrator in *Boomerang* needs to control not only the focus of the narrative, but also the lives of those around him. He lusts after his friends' wives, claiming, "I am a low bastard anyway," and brags about his ability to possess five lovely coeds (*B*, 83). When he loses power within his relationships, he usually abandons his partner and looks for another wife who will succumb more easily to his demands. His self-esteem is tied completely to his ability to conquer those good-looking women whom he meets.

Hannah offers several reasons in *Boomerang* to explain Barry's stubborn need to direct and control those around him. He resents his "uniformly wretched" teachers and blames his parents for the failure of his first marriage: "I will never forgive my parents for not allowing me my life at college, never sticking up for me. They were spineless, discreet. I got home and then married to get away from home" (*B*, 115–16). Although he loves the South, he also sees it as one cause for his narrator's own unreasonably defensive behavior: "We're all so fucking terrible, no wonder it took four years of hideous war to get Lee up there and give up his sword" (*B*, 64). Like the South, Hannah's narrator in *Boomerang* is proud, defensive, and ashamed. Barry's need for control parallels the South's need to exert power over a country that denied it its chosen way of life in the Civil War. Both Barry and the South fight to regain dignity, and both the man and his region expect compensation for a past that cheated them of their self-respect.

According to the narrator, who wears his lack of conscience as a badge in *Boomerang,* he deserves a wife who will tirelessly wait on him while allowing and even encouraging his infidelities. He seems to affect a cocky assuredness more to convince himself of his righteousness than to impress his readers. For example, to describe his wife's increased sexual desire for him and her need for constant oral stimulation, he self-effacingly writes, "I blame myself for being an artist and how awful it might be to miss me" (*B*, 121). And when they argue, she rarely wins: "But I was a wild man and she was fighting for her life. She tried to kick the manhood but it was to no avail. I began strangling her and screaming out the end of Poe's 'Masque of the Red Death'" (*B*, 120). As in previous novels, Hannah's narrator resorts to violence when the capacity to reason no longer works to his advantage, and he blames his past for this admittedly destructive behavior.

But, on the whole, *Boomerang* is Hannah's least violent novel. In fact, Hannah criticizes those countries that use violence as an alternative, those Americans who blithely ignore world politics, and those citizens who overlook the violence that occurs in their own communities. For example, while discussing his trip to Tuscaloosa with Susan, he writes of Arabs who own oil companies and come to America searching for "ignorant" white wives: "One of them came to Ole Miss and has killed both his American wives. They have pride and a certain attitude, you see" (*B*, 79). In the same chapter, he criticizes the ayatollah and the pope for their irresponsi-

ble treatment of children and poverty, and he ends by pointing out the
irony in Michael Jackson's popular song, "We Are the World": "Michael
says God wrote the lyrics. Like God replaced his original face with that of
Diana Ross. But god knows we need our rich phony celebrities" (B, 80).
He even recounts stories of needless violence that once filled the minds of
characters in his earlier novels and provided substance for black comedy.
For example, he tells of a "hideous" man who stabbed another 128 times
over a woman and drugs, more to criticize the lawyer who defended the
killer than to describe the crime. Boomerang represents a subtle change for
Hannah; violence is no longer presented as a reasonable alternative, but as
an inevitable and destructive force in any society.

Although Hannah exhibits a social consciousness in earlier novels, in
Boomerang he also presents a more desperate picture of a degenerating
American society. The only hope he sees lies within the Humane Society,
an organization that he feels stands against needless violence: "I recalled
white country people shooting the forelegs off a dog when they were
through hunting with it, leaving it out to hobble near the highway where
some person might, just might, pick it up and call the Humane Society.
Who in America can ever quit the Humane Society?" (B, 39). He praises
his friend Willie Morris for contributing $140 to the organization, and
criticizes those who irresponsibly ignore the need for animal birth control.
The Humane Society symbolizes in Boomerang the need Hannah recognizes for compassion and support in a period when "Pres. Reagan has
made a lot of shits . . . feel comfortable" (B, 108). Much of what he writes
in Boomerang seems intended to shock readers out of their complacency
and force them to attempt to make a difference, especially within their
own communities. For Hannah, the Humane Society represents one possible starting place.

A second alternative for change Hannah presents in the most fictional
character in his novel, Yelverston, who is to Hannah's narrator in Boomerang what Jack is to Homer in Hey Jack!. The narrator spends much of his
youth fantasizing about a great-uncle named Yelverston, and when he finally meets him (Yelverston is 62 and the narrator is 46), he asks for advice and compassion: "All right, uncle, tell me everything and I will be
your nephew, learning in the new distance. We don't have that many years
to go. Things are shortening up. One of us has got to be wise" (B, 33).
Barton Benton Yelverston, valedictorian of his high school class and
wealthy beyond his expectations, reappears throughout Boomerang much
like Jack in Hey Jack!, and his choices in life make him a perfect role
model and foil for the narrator, who is much less moderate and more

angry than his great-uncle. Barry describes Yelverston as "a man before he was a man" (*B*, 51). He is a good ball player, a loving father, and a capable pilot. Although divorced, Yelverston remains on friendly terms with his ex-wife and "was very satisfied that he had no more envy, sorrow, or littleness in him" (*B*, 56). He sees only the good in people and thinks primarily "of the beauty of anatomy and the holiness of man and human" (*B*, 106). Yelverston is Barry's ideal, the man whom the narrator would like to be.

But like Jack, Yelverston is forced to face the loss of a child: his son is murdered by dope pirates who also wound his daughter-in-law. Yelverston, who had always lived a moderate, peaceful, and healthy life (he had his first drink at 28 and his first Pall Mall at 30), uncharacteristically looks for vengeance. The book chronicles his and his ex-wife Ruth's search for their son's killer, and traces the changes that violence inspires within him. Not only does he begin to drink more heavily, but "there was a fury in him" that was unrecognizable before the violence occurred" (*B*, 99). Yelverston finally discovers that a white alcoholic from Texas named Coresta Haim and his gang of black dope pirates killed his son in a fashion "so vicious and unreasonable it could only be compared to the wild murders of the Hays brothers back in the early days of the Natchez Trail" (*B*, 121). Unlike Jack, however, Yelverston does not wish to take the law into his own hands. He and his wife help the sheriff imprison each of the responsible criminals, which leads to his reunion with his ex-wife. He then becomes complacent with his marriage and his habits (much like Homer in *Hey Jack!*)—five Pall Malls a day and no more than five drinks—and, at 50, Ruth conceives a second son with Yelverston.

In a postscript to the last chapter of *Boomerang*, "Furtherance," Hannah informs readers that "throughout the hate and temporary madness, and the envies and the lack of regard and the calamities that have occurred and all the deaths that have happened as given to us by the mad U.S.A. and the mad god, Yelverston has kept on" (*B*, 143). Like Jack, Yelverston survives. The final picture Hannah offers of Barry's great-uncle is without his wife Ruth, who dies of cancer, but with their son Carl, who represents hope for the future and the possibility of happiness. Yelverston, unlike any other Hannah character, discovers a peaceful solution to his problem. Rather than submit to the violence around him, Yelverston forgives his son's killers, and wreaks his vengeance only by making them face their responsibilities as American citizens and contributing members of a Southern community: he rehabilitates them.

Barry's problems, on the other hand, are not as easily resolved. Although

"Furtherance" indicates that Barry stays with Susan—in fact, he writes her love notes at the hospital where she lies happily "stoned on Nubane" to relieve her migraine and P.M.S. (*B*, 145)—he lies to himself and his readers about their ability to conceive a child: "After three years of trying my wife and I have a new baby coming too. What a lie. We have nothing coming" (*B*, 148). Yelverston offers Barry $3,000 on the condition that he stop smoking and bear a child, but the narrator fails at both challenges. On his last throw of his new boomerang (price now $5.98), Barry is accompanied by Susan, who stays with him, as Barry describes it, "trying not to hate me" (*B*, 140). This time the throw spins evenly and the boomerang returns directly to Barry's clenched fist, reassuring him about his country, his wife, his work, and his friends:

I love the land of the free. I'm standing on soil full of blood and I am still stealing from *me*. Even me, smart, and I've gotten away with it.
   When I get tired of my wife I can dance.
   I can work at the old Smith-Corona she gave me for Father's Day.

I can take my friends fishing and act like an important person. (*B*, 141)

Although Barry cannot lie convincingly about the possibility of permanence between him and Susan, he finds comfort in his friends, his town, and his social consciousness: "We have Oxford and our friends, maybe, all in line, making a defense around Oxford so as to keep the carpetbaggers out" (*B*, 148). The book concludes with Barry joining Yelverston at Ruth's burial. As the narrator describes Yelverston's life, he remains awed at the commitment his great-uncle demonstrates toward those men who killed his son: "In a mansion in Memphis, he has the blacks and Cor Haim around him, taking care of Carl. It's a lifetime deal, he tells me" (*B*, 150). Yelverston not only exhibits faith in the power of rehabilitation, but he places the responsibility for his second son within the hands of those who murdered his first son. For Yelverston, trust and love have the power to initiate change.

   In spite of Barry's inability to emulate his friend Yelverston's tendency to discover peaceful alternatives to combat a violent world, in *Hey Jack!* and *Boomerang* Hannah emphasizes that the needs of the individual are less important that those of the community. Both Homer and Barry find themselves dissatisfied with the violence and corruption that exists within their beloved Mississippi towns, but both recognize that local characters and time-honored traditions have held their communities together.

Hannah's choice of structures for both novels reflects his admiration for the oral tales, passed from generation to generation, that have helped to make sense of history by encouraging its continuity; he emulates the disjunctive nature of storytelling by juxtaposing segments of narrative that heighten the visual quality and seemingly random structure of a well-told story. In both novels he creates an important secondary character whose good sense and compassion provide an alternative to the quick temper and bigotry of the protagonist. Homer and Barry may offer funny, perceptive, critical views of Southern society, but it is Jack and Yelverston who ultimately illustrate that the driving forces of the Southern communities in which they live are faith in the goodness of humankind and a respect for tradition.

Much of this shift in Hannah's perspective can be attributed to his respect for tradition exhibited by his tendency to confront and use honest experience within his novels. In his interview with R. Vanarsdall Hannah discusses his love affair with the English language and the significance of incorporating his own experience in his fiction:

The main thing is that I love the English language very much. That's the one thing I picked up from all the literary study. I just adore it. My kind of affair with the language has gone through a lot of changes. I'm always trying to get as much as I can out of words. That kind of takes over. You're faithful to experience and you try that with words, you really don't have a lot of time to think about audience. Just a kind of wise person who might be enjoying some of the experience with you. (341)

In all of his fiction, from *Geronimo Rex* to *Boomerang,* Hannah attempts to share much of his personal experience. Autobiographical incident serves as the basis for each of his works, but as he progresses as a writer, he experiments with fictional form to discover new methods of expressing his frustrations with and love for the South and its people. From the violent and impulsive Harriman Monroe to the philosophical and reflective "Barry," Hannah emphasizes in his fiction his characters' need to strike an acceptable balance within their lives, to retain spontaneity without dismissing their responsibilities as community members.

As Hannah grows older, his characters reflect an impatience with the easy solution. Figures such as Jack and Yelverston, absent in his earlier works, represent "ideals," characters who may realistically succumb to the seductive nature of violence and dishonesty, but who ultimately overcome these destructive impulses. As his novels grow more autobiographical and introspective, Hannah experiments with form to imitate the visual and associational nature of memory and the random structure of the mind. His later works contain fewer references to the Civil and Vietnam wars, and actual people with whom Hannah has come into contact replace the Jeb Stuarts and Robert E. Lees of the earlier fiction. In *Hey Jack!* and *Boomerang* he illustrates a new direction for his future works, one that openly expresses autobiographical incident as a means to reevaluate the lives of his protagonists. In his more recent fiction, the needs of the individual are subordinated to the needs of the community. Hannah implies that only through this emphasis on the values of the community can the South preserve the traditions that it, and Hannah, hold dear.

Notes and References

Chapter One

1. R. Vanarsdall, "The Spirits Will Win Through: An Interview with Barry Hannah," *Southern Review* 19 (1983): 339; hereafter cited in text.
2. Jan Gretland, "Interview with Barry Hannah," *Contemporary Authors* 110 (1984): 233; hereafter cited in text.
3. David Madden, "Barry Hannah's *Geronimo Rex* in Retrospect," *Southern Review* 19 (1983): 310; hereafter cited in text.
4. John Updike, "From Dyna Domes to Turkey-Pressing," review of *Geronimo Rex, New Yorker,* 121; hereafter cited in text.
5. Jim Harrison, "Three Novels: Comic, Cute, Cool," review of *Geronimo Rex, New York Times Book Review,* 14 May 1972, 4; hereafter cited in text.
6. *Geronimo Rex* (New York: Penguin Books, 1987), 36; hereafter cited in text as *Rex.*
7. Donald R. Noble, " 'Tragic and Meaningful to an Insane Degree': Barry Hannah," *Southern Literary Journal* 15, no. 1 (1982): 40; hereafter cited in text.
8. Robert W. Hill, "Barry Hannah," *South Carolina Review* 9, no. 1 (1976): 28; hereafter cited in text.
9. Jonathan Yardley, "Love and Death and Points in Between," review of *Nightwatchmen, New York Times Book Review,* 18 November 1973, 34; hereafter cited in text.
10. Arnold Asrelsky, review of *Nightwatchmen, Library Journal* 98 (1973): 2880.
11. John Skow, "Pain and Fancy: *Nightwatchmen," Book World—Washington Post,* 23 December 1973, 3; hereafter cited in text.
12. Charles Israel, "Barry Hannah," in *Dictionary of Literary Biography: American Novelists since World War II,* 2d ser., vol. 6 ed. James E. Kibler, Jr. (Detroit: Gale Research Co., 1980), 132; hereafter cited in text.
13. *Nightwatchmen* (New York: Viking Press, 1973), 42; hereafter cited in text as *NW.*

Chapter Two

1. *Airships* (New York: Vintage Contemporaries, 1985), 4; hereafter cited in text as *A.*
2. Allen Shepherd, "Outrage and Speculation: Barry Hannah's *Airships," Notes on Mississippi Writers* 14, no. 2 (1982): 63; hereafter cited in text.
3. Michael Malone, "Everything That Rises," *Nation,* 10 June 1978, 705; hereafter cited in text.

4. George M. Kelly, review of *Airships,* by Barry Hannah, *Library Journal* 103 (1978): 1081; hereafter cited in text.

5. Michael Wood, "Southern Comforts," *New York Times Book Review,* 23 April 1978, 1, 35; hereafter cited in text.

6. Robert Towers, "Forced Marches," *New York Review of Books,* 15 June 1978, 29–30.

Chapter Three

1. Eliot Fremont-Smith, "Hoo-Ray," review of *Ray, Village Voice,* 19 November 1980, 45; hereafter cited in text.

2. *Ray* (New York: Penguin Books, 1980), 4; hereafter cited in text as *Ray.*

3. Harry Crews, "Carry on, Doctor," *Book World: Washington Post,* 16 November 1980, 4; hereafter cited in text.

4. Walter Clemons, "Talk Show," *Newsweek,* 15 December 1980, 100; hereafter cited in text.

5. Benjamin DeMott, "Rudeness Is Our Only Hope," *New York Times Book Review,* 16 November 1980, 7; hereafter cited in text.

6. Michael Malone, "A Southern Ray of Hope," *Nation,* 29 November 1980, 585; hereafter cited in text.

7. Geoffrey Wolff, "Answering the Old World," *New Republic,* 13 December 1980, 31; hereafter cited in text.

8. *The Tennis Handsome* (New York: Charles Scribner's and Sons, 1987), 14; hereafter cited in text as *TH.*

9. Jack Beatty, review of *The Tennis Handsome, New Republic,* 18 April 1983, 39; hereafter cited in text.

10. Ivan Gold, "Yoknapatawpha County of the Mind," review of *The Tennis Handsome, New York Times Book Review,* 1 May 1983, 11; hereafter cited in text.

11. W. B. H., review of *The Tennis Handsome, Booklist* 79 (1983): 945; hereafter cited in text.

12. Review of *The Tennis Handsome,* by Barry Hannah, *Time,* 4 July 1983, 70; hereafter cited in text.

13. Christopher Lehmann-Haupt, review of *The Tennis Handsome, New York Times,* 18 April 1983, C–15; hereafter cited in text.

Chapter Four

1. Terrence Rafferty, "Gunsmoke and Voodoo," *Nation* 1 June 1985, 679; hereafter cited in text.

2. James Wolcott, "Southern Discomfort," *New York Times Review of Books,* 27 June 1985, 33; hereafter cited in text.

3. Christopher Lehmann-Haupt, "Books of the Times," review of *Captain Maximus, New York Times,* 29 April 1985, C–18; hereafter cited in text.

4. *Captain Maximus* (New York: Alfred A. Knopf, 1985), 4; hereafter cited in text as *CM.*

5. Raymond Federman, *Surfiction: Fiction Now . . . and Tomorrow* (Chicago: Swallow Press, 1975), 3; hereafter cited in text.

6. Ronald Sukenick, *In Form: Digressions on the Art of Fiction* (Carbondale: Southern Illinois University Press, 1985), ix; hereafter cited in text.

7. Doris Betts, "Barry Hannah: Where Energy Is All," *Book World— Washington Post,* 23 June 1985, 11; hereafter cited in text.

8. George Stade, "Lives of Noisy Desperation," *New York Times Book Review,* 9 June 1985, 14; hereafter cited in text.

9. Allen G. Shepherd III, "The Latest Whiz Bang: Barry Hannah's *Captain Maximus," Notes on Mississippi Writers* 19, no. 1 (1987): 33; hereafter cited in text.

10. Sergei Eisenstein, *Film Form,* ed. and trans. Jay Leyda (New York: Harcourt, Brace, and World, 1949), 93; hereafter cited in text.

Chapter Five

1. *Hey Jack!* (New York: E. P. Dutton-Seymour Lawrence, 1987), 1–2; hereafter cited in text as *HJ.*

2. Albert E. Wilhelm, review of *Hey Jack!, Library Journal* 112 (1987); 108; hereafter cited in text.

3. Michiko Kakutani, "Books of the Times," review of *Hey Jack!, New York Times,* 18 Nov. 1987, C–33; hereafter cited in text.

4. Thomas R. Edwards, "Stolen Loves, Manly Vengeance," *New Times Book Review,* 1 November 1987, 26; hereafter cited in text.

5. Jim Kobak, review of *Hey Jack!, Kirkus Review* 55 (1987): 950; hereafter cited in text.

6. Richard Eder, "A War Memorial in the Mind," *Book Review—Los Angeles Times,* 6 September 1987, 12; hereafter cited in text.

7. *Boomerang* (Boston: Houghton Mifflin, 1989); hereafter cited in text as *B.*

8. Sybil Steinberg, review of *Boomerang, Publishers Weekly* 235 (1989): 57; hereafter cited in text.

9. Joanna Kennedy, review of *Boomerang, New York Times Book Review,* 14 April 1989, 19; hereafter cited in text.

Selected Bibliography

PRIMARY WORKS

Airships. New York: Alfred A. Knopf, 1978.

Boomerang. Boston: Houghton Mifflin/Seymour Lawrence, 1989.

Captain Maximus. New York: Alfred A. Knopf, 1985.

Geronimo Rex. New York: Viking Press, 1972.

Hey Jack! New York: E. P. Dutton/Seymour Lawrence, 1987.

Nightwatchmen. New York: Viking Press, 1973.

Ray. New York: Alfred A. Knopf, 1980.

The Tennis Handsome. New York: Alfred A. Knopf, 1983.

SECONDARY WORKS

Crews, Harry. "Carry on, Doctor." Review of *Ray. Book World: Washington Post,* 16 November 1980. "In this novel, there are no transitions of time or space, but what emerges is a narrative that has the kind of unity and coherence that we associate with the best fiction."

DeMott, Benjamin. "Rudeness Is Our Only Hope." Review of *Ray. New York Times Book Review,* 16 November 1980, 7, 26. "The trouble is that, while *Ray* is the funniest, weirdest, soul-happiest work of fiction by a genuinely young American author that I've read in a long while, ordinary reviewerese is no help in explaining why."

Eder, Richard. "A War Memorial in the Mind." Review of *Hey Jack! Book Review—Los Angeles Times,* 6 September 1987, 3, 12. "Homer's wandering cogitations, his tales, his pleasures, and his anguish all ramble to a purpose. They test and reveal the tensile strength of a cord that is never really loosed; that binds him to his deadly memories, that binds his Southern communities and perhaps all communities to their own."

Edwards, Thomas R. "Stolen Loves, Manly Vengeance." Review of *Hey Jack! New York Times Book Review,* 1 November 1987, 26. "But in his new novella, *Hey Jack!,* geography, local culture, and a sense of his precursors—especially Faulkner—seem to be interfering with his performance."

Gold, Ivan. "Yoknapatawpha County of the Mind." Review of *The Tennis Handsome. New York Times Book Review,* 1 May 1983, 11, 19. "While *The Tennis*

Handsome may not be his 'best book' already assembled or yet to come, it's as good a place to start reading Barry Hannah as any. He is an original, or if names are to be dropped, Carson McCullers rewritten by Groucho Marx."

Gretland, Jan. "Interview with Barry Hannah." *Contemporary Authors* 110 (1984): 233–239. An insightful interview with Hannah about violence, music, writing, teaching, and literature. Good source for biographical information.

Halio, Jay L. "Violence and After." *Southern Review* 15 (July 1979): 702–710. Includes interesting discussion of Hannah's use of war brutalities and grotesques.

Hill, Robert W. "Barry Hannah," *South Carolina Review* 9, no. 1 (1976): 25–29. Describes Hannah as a stylist and satirist. Cites major theme of affirmation in his works.

Israel, Charles. "Barry Hannah." In *Dictionary of Literary Biography: American Novelists Since World War II,* 2d ser., vol. 6, edited by James E. Kibler, Jr., 131–33. Detroit: Gale Research Co., 1980. Traces Hannah's treatment of the South as microcosm for universal human condition in his early works.

Jones, John Griffith. "Interview with Barry Hannah." In *Mississippi Writers Talking.* Jackson: University Press of Mississippi, 1982. Interview with Hannah that includes discussion of language, themes, and screenplays.

Kakutani, Michiko. "Books of the Times." Review of *Hey Jack!, New York Times,* 18 November 1987, C–33. "There is little affection, generosity or understanding in Homer's—or, for that matter, Mr. Hannah's—depiction of these people; and, as a result, they seem a random collection of misfits whose eccentricity, selfishness and stupidity mean nothing."

Madden, David. "Barry Hannah's *Geronimo Rex* in Retrospect." *Southern Review* 19 (1983): 309–16. Reevaluation of *Geronimo Rex,* praising Hannah for style and use of language and criticizing him for his inability to develop character or sustain continuity.

Malone, Michael. "A Southern Ray of Hope." Review of *Ray. Nation,* 29 November 1980, 585–86. "The result is very writerly speaking, an exhilarating verbal explosion of excess, that nobody in bland stumbling life speaks—except maybe a few Southerners like Senator Sam Ervin."

Noble, Donald R. " 'Tragic and Meaningful to an Insane Degree': Barry Hannah." *Southern Literary Journal* 15, no. 1 (1982): 37–44. Explains depth of comic vision and significance of music, violence, and chaos in early works through *Ray.* Defines Hannah as antinihilistic. Sees Hannah's use of voice and language as his greatest gift.

Rafferty, Terrence. "Gunsmoke and Voodoo." Review of *Captain Maximus. Nation* 240 (1985): 677–79. "What Hannah does with his own feelings is what he does with all elements of his fiction, historical or imagined: He transforms them into private myths."

Shepherd, Allen. "Outrage and Speculation: Barry Hannah's *Airships." Notes on Mississippi Writers* 14, no. 2 (1982): 63–73. Insightful and detailed analysis of many of the stories and major themes in *Airships*. Praises Hannah for his perfect dialogue, poetic metaphors, and carefully worked out symbols.

Shepherd, Allen G., III. "The Latest Whiz Bang: Barry Hannah's *Captain Maximus*." *Notes on Mississippi Writers* 19, no. 1 (1987): 29–33. Criticizes Hannah's inability to sustain narrative interest and generate original subject matter in *Captain Maximus*.

Stade, George. "Lives of Noisy Desperation." Review of *Captain Maximus*. *New York Times Book Review*, 9 June 1985, 14. "And that is how the other stories in *Captain Maximus* rush out to us, on the shock and thud of metaphor, the sentences abrupt, the silences between them full of menace."

Towers, Robert. "Forced Marches." Review of *Airships*. *New York Review of Books*, 15 June 1978, 29–30. "Though Hannah's narrative excesses are in evidence throughout, several scenes are so beautifully mounted and sustained that they briefly (too briefly) exalt his artistry to the level we associate with Eudora Welty and Flannery O'Connor."

Updike, John. "From Dyna-Domes to Turkey Pressing." Review of *Geronimo Rex*. *New Yorker*, 9 September 1972, 115–24. "The major weakness of a first novel like this is its limp susceptibility to autobiographical accident; its vitality must lie not in the shaping but in the language of the telling, and here Mr. Hannah is no mean performer."

Vanarsdall, R. "The Spirits Will Win Through: An Interview with Barry Hannah." *Southern Review* 19 (1983): 314–41. Most revealing interview with Hannah to date. The author discusses autobiographical sources for early works; the influence of writers such as Henry Miller and Thomas Wolfe upon his own writing; his fascination with violence and danger; his problems with alcohol; his work in California as a screenwriter; and his love of music.

Wolcott, James. "Southern Discomfort." Review of *Captain Maximus*. *New York Times*, 29 April 1985, 33–34. "At his best, Barry Hannah has a quirky command of the language, a light-fingered delight in the absurd; he's one of the few short-story writers around who refuse to paint the world in shades of gray."

Wood, Michael. "Southern Comforts." Review of *Airships*. *New York Times Book Review*, 23 April 1978, 1, 35. "Mr. Hannah not only has a voice of his own, but a precise, personal inflection. There is a kinship with Eudora Welty, perhaps, or Flannery O'Connor—an eccentric response to a world of fading but rigid social convention—but Mr. Hannah's style is more abrupt."

Yardley, Jonathan. "Love and Death and Points in Between." Review of *Nightwatchmen*. *New York Review*, 18 November 1973, 14. "*Nightwatchmen* attempts to be a consideration of love and death and points in between, but it sustains so little narrative interest that its unastonishing conclusions are scarcely worth the labor of reaching them."

Index

The Author

Mark Jay Charney received his B.A. from Clemson University, his M.A. from the University of New Orleans, and his Ph.D in English from Tulane University in New Orleans. He is currently an associate professor teaching contemporary American literature, film studies, and technical writing at Clemson University in South Carolina, where he also chairs Five Directions, the university's alternative film club. In July 1991 he will serve as assistant head of the Department of English at Clemson University. He has written articles on film adaptations of works by Ernest Gaines, the relationship of the postcontemporary novel to the cinema, and various pedagogical methods of teaching writing. He is currently working on a biography of D. W. Griffith for the University Press of Virginia's Minds of the New South Intellectual Biography Series.

The Editor

Frank Day is a professor of English at Clemson University. He is the author of *Sir William Empson: An Annotated Bibliography* and *Arthur Koestler: A Guide to Research.* He was a Fulbright Lecturer in American Literature in Romania (1980–81) and in Bangladesh (1986–87).